LONG DIVISION
WORKBOOK

Included

Grade 4

The steps

÷ Divide

× Multiply

- Subtract

√ Check

↓ Bring down

↺ Repeat or

R Remainder

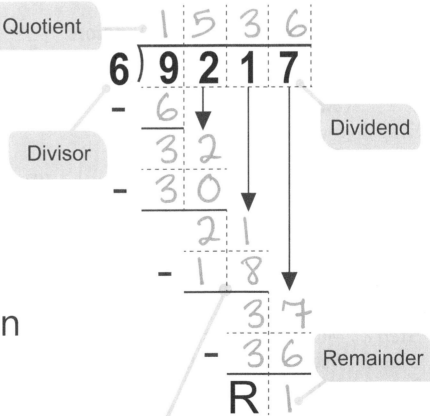

Quotient

Divisor

Dividend

Remainder

The scaffolded steps help the children to arrange the numbers in the correct columns to get the right answers

@MathematicsByKim

Contents

Steps for Long Division

Step 1 : Ask: How many groups of 4 can I get out of 9?
     Tow times because 4 times **2** is **8**.
Step 2 : Multiply: **2 × 4 = 8**.
Step 3 : Subtract: **9 – 8 = 1**.
Step 4 : Bring down the next place value (**8**).

Repeat the steps

Step 1 : Ask: How many groups of 4 can I get out of **18**?
     4 times because **4** times **4** is **16**.
Step 2 : Multiply: **4 × 4 = 16**.
Step 3 : Subtract: **18 – 16 = 2**.
Remainder is **2**.

$$4\overline{)98} = 24\,R\,2$$

@MathematicsByKim

♪Long Division
★ Level 0
★ 2-Digit dividends
★ No remainder

Date: ....

Name: ....

Score: ...... /16

☆1 $2\overline{)9\,2}$	☆2 $5\overline{)8\,5}$	☆3 $3\overline{)8\,1}$	☆4 $5\overline{)8\,0}$
☆5 $7\overline{)7\,0}$	☆6 $4\overline{)9\,2}$	☆7 $7\overline{)8\,4}$	☆8 $7\overline{)7\,7}$
☆9 $4\overline{)8\,0}$	☆10 $4\overline{)9\,6}$	☆11 $5\overline{)7\,5}$	☆12 $6\overline{)9\,0}$
☆13 $4\overline{)9\,2}$	☆14 $6\overline{)7\,2}$	☆15 $3\overline{)9\,0}$	☆16 $3\overline{)8\,7}$

Long Division

★ Level 0
★ 2-Digit dividends
★ No remainder

Date: ....

Name: ....

Score: ...... /16

1

$3\overline{)6\,9}$

$-\underline{}\downarrow$

$-$

R

2

$5\overline{)8\,5}$

$-\underline{}\downarrow$

$-$

R

3

$4\overline{)7\,6}$

$-\underline{}\downarrow$

$-$

R

4

$3\overline{)6\,9}$

$-\underline{}\downarrow$

$-$

R

5

$5\overline{)9\,0}$

$-\underline{}\downarrow$

$-$

R

6

$3\overline{)9\,0}$

$-\underline{}\downarrow$

$-$

R

7

$4\overline{)8\,4}$

$-\underline{}\downarrow$

$-$

R

8

$3\overline{)8\,1}$

$-\underline{}\downarrow$

$-$

R

9

$6\overline{)9\,0}$

$-\underline{}\downarrow$

$-$

R

10

$4\overline{)8\,4}$

$-\underline{}\downarrow$

$-$

R

11

$3\overline{)9\,3}$

$-\underline{}\downarrow$

$-$

R

12

$5\overline{)9\,5}$

$-\underline{}\downarrow$

$-$

R

13

$7\overline{)7\,7}$

$-\underline{}\downarrow$

$-$

R

14

$4\overline{)8\,0}$

$-\underline{}\downarrow$

$-$

R

15

$5\overline{)7\,5}$

$-\underline{}\downarrow$

$-$

R

16

$3\overline{)9\,3}$

$-\underline{}\downarrow$

$-$

R

Long Division

★ Level 0
★ 2-Digit dividends
★ No remainder

Date: ....

Name: ....

Score: ...... /16

1	2	3	4
3)93 — — R	6)78 — — R	3)69 — — R	6)72 — — R

5	6	7	8
5)85 — — R	5)90 — — R	4)76 — — R	7)70 — — R

9	10	11	12
7)91 — — R	3)90 — — R	5)90 — — R	4)76 — — R

13	14	15	16
5)85 — — R	2)96 — — R	4)88 — — R	3)81 — — R

) Long Division
★ Level 0
★ 2-Digit dividends
★ With remainder

Date: ....

Name: ....

Score: ...... /16

1
```
       2 4
   4 ) 9 9
   -   8 ↓
       1 9
   -   1 6
     R   3
```

2
```
   6 ) 9 3
   -       ↓
   -
       R
```

3
```
   5 ) 7 2
   -       ↓
   -
       R
```

4
```
   4 ) 8 2
   -       ↓
   -
       R
```

5
```
   6 ) 8 9
   -     ↓
   -
     R
```

6
```
   5 ) 9 9
   -       ↓
   -
       R
```

7
```
   5 ) 9 4
   -       ↓
   -
       R
```

8
```
   4 ) 8 3
   -       ↓
   -
       R
```

9
```
   6 ) 7 6
   -     ↓
   -
     R
```

10
```
   3 ) 7 8
   -       ↓
   -
       R
```

11
```
   6 ) 9 8
   -       ↓
   -
       R
```

12
```
   5 ) 9 1
   -       ↓
   -
       R
```

13
```
   5 ) 7 4
   -     ↓
   -
       R
```

14
```
   2 ) 9 4
   -       ↓
   -
       R
```

15
```
   3 ) 7 7
   -     ↓
   -
       R
```

16
```
   5 ) 8 8
   -     ↓
   -
       R
```

Long Division

★ Level 0
★ 2-Digit dividends
★ With remainder

Date: ....

Name: ....

Score: ...... /16

1 $7\overline{)79}$ R	**2** $2\overline{)82}$ R	**3** $5\overline{)77}$ R	**4** $6\overline{)81}$ R
5 $5\overline{)96}$ R	**6** $2\overline{)91}$ R	**7** $3\overline{)85}$ R	**8** $5\overline{)83}$ R
9 $6\overline{)80}$ R	**10** $2\overline{)78}$ R	**11** $4\overline{)86}$ R	**12** $3\overline{)92}$ R
13 $5\overline{)74}$ R	**14** $4\overline{)74}$ R	**15** $4\overline{)71}$ R	**16** $4\overline{)76}$ R

Long Division

★ Level 0
★ 2-Digit dividends
★ With remainder

Date: ....

Name: ....

Score: ...... /16

1	2	3	4
$7\overline{)95}$	$3\overline{)85}$	$7\overline{)85}$	$7\overline{)90}$
5	6	7	8
$2\overline{)83}$	$5\overline{)80}$	$3\overline{)96}$	$2\overline{)95}$
9	10	11	12
$3\overline{)75}$	$3\overline{)86}$	$6\overline{)78}$	$3\overline{)80}$
13	14	15	16
$2\overline{)99}$	$6\overline{)95}$	$6\overline{)82}$	$6\overline{)94}$

)Long Division
★ Level 0
★ 2-Digit dividends
★ With remainder

Date: ....

Name: ....

Score: ...... /16

1	7)80	2	5)79	3	4)85	4	4)95

5	4)73	6	6)93	7	3)77	8	6)96

9	7)92	10	5)71	11	7)77	12	4)75

13	5)75	14	4)72	15	5)77	16	2)76

) Long Division
★ Level 0
★ 2-Digit dividends
★ With remainder

Date: ....

Name: ....

Score: ...... /16

1 6)90
   - __ ↓
   - -----
   ____ R

2 3)72
   - __ ↓
   - -----
   ____ R

3 5)89
   - __ ↓
   - -----
   ____ R

4 7)96
   - __ ↓
   - -----
   ____ R

5 7)73
   - __ ↓
   - -----
   ____ R

6 4)76
   - __ ↓
   - -----
   ____ R

7 3)76
   - __ ↓
   - -----
   ____ R

8 5)82
   - __ ↓
   - -----
   ____ R

9 4)88
   - __ ↓
   - -----
   ____ R

10 7)90
   - __ ↓
   - -----
   ____ R

11 4)89
   - __ ↓
   - -----
   ____ R

12 4)94
   - __ ↓
   - -----
   ____ R

13 6)78
   - __ ↓
   - -----
   ____ R

14 2)89
   - __ ↓
   - -----
   ____ R

15 3)91
   - __ ↓
   - -----
   ____ R

16 3)83
   - __ ↓
   - -----
   ____ R

Long Division

★ Level 1
★ 3-Digit dividends
★ No remainder

Date: ....

Name: ....

Score: ...... /16

1	2	3	4
4) 9 0 4	5) 7 7 0	5) 7 6 0	6) 7 1 4
5	6	7	8
5) 7 3 5	6) 9 6 6	7) 9 3 1	4) 9 9 2
9	10	11	12
6) 9 8 4	7) 9 0 3	6) 8 6 4	5) 9 7 0
13	14	15	16
4) 7 8 0	4) 8 4 0	3) 7 3 2	6) 9 4 8

Long Division

★ Level 1
★ 3-Digit dividends
★ No remainder

Date: ....

Name: ....

Score: ...... /16

1 $3\overline{)975}$	**2** $6\overline{)762}$	**3** $2\overline{)810}$	**4** $2\overline{)884}$
5 $4\overline{)716}$	**6** $6\overline{)708}$	**7** $5\overline{)755}$	**8** $4\overline{)848}$
9 $3\overline{)771}$	**10** $4\overline{)800}$	**11** $6\overline{)786}$	**12** $3\overline{)993}$
13 $7\overline{)847}$	**14** $4\overline{)880}$	**15** $5\overline{)800}$	**16** $2\overline{)824}$

Long Division

★ Level 1
★ 3-Digit dividends
★ No remainder

Date: ....

Name: ....

Score: ...... /16

1 $5\overline{)715}$	**2** $4\overline{)852}$	**3** $3\overline{)747}$	**4** $2\overline{)848}$
5 $6\overline{)750}$	**6** $4\overline{)916}$	**7** $3\overline{)822}$	**8** $4\overline{)844}$
9 $2\overline{)936}$	**10** $5\overline{)935}$	**11** $6\overline{)786}$	**12** $5\overline{)895}$
13 $5\overline{)905}$	**14** $6\overline{)822}$	**15** $6\overline{)882}$	**16** $6\overline{)918}$

Long Division

★ Level 1
★ 3-Digit dividends
★ No remainder

Date: ....

Name: ....

Score: ...... /16

1 6) 8 2 2   R

2 4) 9 3 2   R

3 3) 7 1 4   R

4 5) 7 9 5   R

5 4) 8 7 6   R

6 3) 7 5 6   R

7 3) 8 5 5   R

8 5) 8 7 5   R

9 4) 9 6 8   R

10 5) 7 8 5   R

11 6) 7 9 8   R

12 6) 8 1 0   R

13 3) 8 7 6   R

14 4) 9 0 8   R

15 6) 7 2 0   R

16 6) 9 1 2   R

Long Division

★ Level 1
★ 3-Digit dividends
★ No remainder

Date: ....

Name: ....

Score: ...... /16

1	$2\overline{)740}$
2	$4\overline{)836}$
3	$6\overline{)822}$
4	$3\overline{)975}$

5	$6\overline{)960}$
6	$7\overline{)931}$
7	$7\overline{)861}$
8	$5\overline{)745}$

9	$3\overline{)831}$
10	$3\overline{)834}$
11	$5\overline{)810}$
12	$2\overline{)882}$

13	$7\overline{)847}$
14	$7\overline{)945}$
15	$3\overline{)783}$
16	$5\overline{)855}$

Long Division

★ Level 1
★ 3-Digit dividends
★ No remainder

Name: ....

1	2	3	4
6)864	7)763	4)800	5)855
R	R	R	R

5	6	7	8
6)804	4)820	6)930	4)736
R	R	R	R

9	10	11	12
2)756	2)792	4)836	7)910
R	R	R	R

13	14	15	16
6)900	4)984	3)750	5)935
R	R	R	R

Long Division

★ Level 1
★ 3-Digit dividends
★ No remainder

Date: ....

Name: ....

Score: ...... /16

1	2	3	4
6) 8 1 0	3) 7 7 4	4) 9 1 2	2) 8 2 4
R	R	R	R

5	6	7	8
2) 9 2 0	4) 8 8 0	4) 9 7 2	7) 8 4 7
R	R	R	R

9	10	11	12
5) 9 2 5	3) 8 9 7	5) 8 3 5	6) 9 9 0
R	R	R	R

13	14	15	16
3) 8 8 8	5) 7 5 5	3) 9 0 6	5) 8 6 0
R	R	R	R

Long Division

★ Level 1
★ 3-Digit dividends
★ No remainder

Date: ....

Name: ....

Score: ...... /16

1) $3\overline{)870}$	2) $3\overline{)891}$	3) $5\overline{)820}$	4) $4\overline{)936}$
5) $4\overline{)708}$	6) $2\overline{)912}$	7) $7\overline{)707}$	8) $4\overline{)748}$
9) $7\overline{)854}$	10) $3\overline{)738}$	11) $4\overline{)844}$	12) $4\overline{)796}$
13) $7\overline{)938}$	14) $5\overline{)860}$	15) $3\overline{)861}$	16) $6\overline{)702}$

Long Division

★ Level 1
★ 3-Digit dividends
★ No remainder

Date: ....

Name: ....

Score: ...... /16

1 7)973
R

2 5)735
R

3 4)988
R

4 4)800
R

5 2)950
R

6 7)756
R

7 6)834
R

8 4)756
R

9 5)825
R

10 7)889
R

11 5)715
R

12 5)705
R

13 5)850
R

14 4)960
R

15 2)778
R

16 6)750
R

Long Division
★ Level 1
★ 3-Digit dividends
★ No remainder

Date: ....

Name: ....

Score: ...... /16

1	2	3	4
3)927	6)870	4)716	4)848
5	6	7	8
7)700	6)948	7)917	3)774
9	10	11	12
2)790	3)912	7)987	4)936
13	14	15	16
6)984	3)864	4)940	5)965

Long Division

★ Level 1
★ 3-Digit dividends
★ No remainder

Date: ....

Name: ....

Score: ...... /16

1 3) 5 1 6 — R

2 4) 4 6 0 — R

3 2) 5 6 8 — R

4 3) 5 0 4 — R

5 4) 6 6 8 — R

6 3) 5 5 2 — R

7 3) 6 3 3 — R

8 4) 6 9 6 — R

9 2) 4 3 0 — R

10 4) 4 7 2 — R

11 2) 6 7 4 — R

12 4) 5 3 2 — R

13 3) 5 4 0 — R

14 3) 6 7 8 — R

15 4) 6 4 4 — R

16 3) 6 3 6 — R

Long Division

★ Level 1
★ 3-Digit dividends
★ No remainder

Date: ....

Name: ....

Score: ...... /16

1	2	3	4
4)472	2)444	2)504	2)478
5	6	7	8
3)504	2)400	2)628	2)596
9	10	11	12
3)648	3)627	2)580	3)615
13	14	15	16
3)693	3)426	3)546	3)681

Long Division
★ Level 1
★ 3-Digit dividends
★ No remainder

Date: ....

Name: ....

Score: ...... /16

1 3)666
−
R

2 4)432
−
R

3 3)606
−
R

4 2)562
−
R

5 4)616
−
R

6 3)630
−
R

7 2)442
−
R

8 4)416
−
R

9 2)496
−
R

10 4)604
−
R

11 3)549
−
R

12 2)654
−
R

13 4)480
−
R

14 3)576
−
R

15 3)681
−
R

16 2)456
−
R

♪ Long Division
★ Level 1
★ 3-Digit dividends
★ No remainder

Date: ....

Name: ....

Score: ...... /16

① 3)657
R

② 3)486
R

③ 2)460
R

④ 3)399
R

⑤ 3)483
R

⑥ 3)618
R

⑦ 2)602
R

⑧ 2)684
R

⑨ 3)543
R

⑩ 4)412
R

⑪ 3)639
R

⑫ 4)444
R

⑬ 4)616
R

⑭ 3)507
R

⑮ 3)474
R

⑯ 4)436
R

Long Division

★ Level 1
★ 3-Digit dividends
★ No remainder

Date: ....

Name: ....

Score: ...... /16

1	2	3	4
6) 7 6 8	6) 7 0 8	5) 7 4 0	6) 7 4 4
5	6	7	8
7) 7 0 7	5) 7 4 0	7) 7 4 2	7) 7 3 5
9	10	11	12
5) 7 0 5	6) 7 8 0	7) 7 2 1	7) 7 0 7
13	14	15	16
7) 7 4 9	6) 7 2 6	7) 7 3 5	5) 7 5 5

Long Division
★ Level 1
★ 3-Digit dividends
★ No remainder

Date: ....

Name: ....

Score: ...... /16

1) 8)848 R

2) 8)864 R

3) 8)832 R

4) 7)889 R

5) 6)894 R

6) 7)861 R

7) 6)894 R

8) 6)798 R

9) 7)889 R

10) 7)882 R

11) 8)888 R

12) 7)826 R

13) 6)804 R

14) 6)804 R

15) 7)889 R

16) 8)896 R

Long Division

★ Level 1
★ 3-Digit dividends
★ No remainder

Date: ....

Name: ....

Score: ...... /16

1	2	3	4
8)920	9)918	9)900	8)936
R	R	R	R

5	6	7	8
7)931	7)973	7)966	8)912
R	R	R	R

9	10	11	12
8)984	8)936	7)959	8)968
R	R	R	R

13	14	15	16
7)924	9)990	9)927	7)952
R	R	R	R

Long Division

★ Level 2
★ 3-Digit dividends
★ With remainder

Date: ....

Name: ....

Score: ...... /16

1 6) 8 6 2 R	**2** 3) 9 9 5 R	**3** 7) 8 4 1 R	**4** 7) 9 3 5 R
5 6) 9 7 0 R	**6** 5) 9 4 6 R	**7** 2) 9 1 1 R	**8** 5) 7 6 9 R
9 3) 9 9 2 R	**10** 5) 8 2 8 R	**11** 4) 9 3 0 R	**12** 4) 7 2 0 R
13 5) 9 4 0 R	**14** 5) 7 2 4 R	**15** 4) 9 2 7 R	**16** 3) 7 9 4 R

Long Division

★ Level 2
★ 3-Digit dividends
★ With remainder

Date: ....

Name: ....

Score: ...... /16

1) 6)981 − − − R

2) 4)744 − − R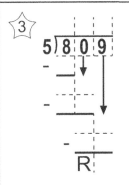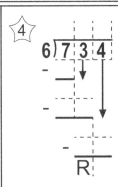

3) 5)809 − − R

4) 6)734 − − R

5) 5)958 − − R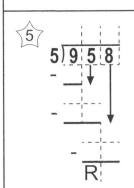

6) 6)988 − − R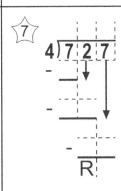

7) 4)727 − − R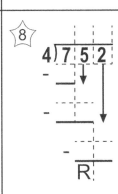

8) 4)752 − − R

9) 6)914 − − R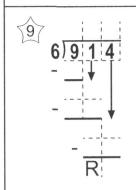

10) 4)911 − − R

11) 6)964 − − R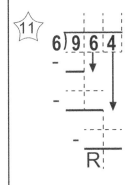

12) 5)969 − − R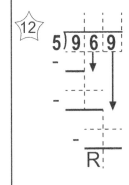

13) 2)996 − − R

14) 5)742 − − R

15) 3)789 − − R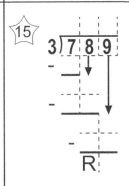

16) 2)737 − − R

Long Division
★ Level 2
★ 3-Digit dividends
★ With remainder

Date: ....

Name: ....

Score: ...... /16

1) $2\overline{)979}$ R

2) $2\overline{)963}$ R

3) $2\overline{)987}$ R

4) $4\overline{)786}$ R

5) $3\overline{)908}$ R

6) $4\overline{)753}$ R

7) $6\overline{)755}$ R

8) $4\overline{)978}$ R

9) $7\overline{)801}$ R

10) $3\overline{)780}$ R

11) $4\overline{)958}$ R

12) $5\overline{)710}$ R

13) $5\overline{)805}$ R

14) $6\overline{)955}$ R

15) $2\overline{)833}$ R

16) $2\overline{)820}$ R

Long Division

★ Level 2
★ 3-Digit dividends
★ With remainder

Date: ....

Name: ....

Score: ...... /16

1 6)981
R

2 7)752
R

3 3)853
R

4 2)859
R

5 3)869
R

6 5)910
R

7 3)897
R

8 6)906
R

9 4)974
R

10 5)952
R

11 5)866
R

12 6)892
R

13 3)893
R

14 3)718
R

15 4)961
R

16 5)780
R

@MathematicsByKim

-31-

Long Division
★ Level 2
★ 3-Digit dividends
★ With remainder

Date: ....

Name: ....

Score: ...... /16

1 $4\overline{)755}$ R

2 $3\overline{)886}$ R

3 $6\overline{)770}$ R

4 $7\overline{)941}$ R

5 $3\overline{)959}$ R

6 $6\overline{)946}$ R

7 $6\overline{)706}$ R

8 $3\overline{)962}$ R

9 $4\overline{)896}$ R

10 $3\overline{)720}$ R

11 $7\overline{)799}$ R

12 $6\overline{)910}$ R

13 $5\overline{)750}$ R

14 $4\overline{)909}$ R

15 $4\overline{)837}$ R

16 $7\overline{)811}$ R

Long Division

★ Level 2
★ 3-Digit dividends
★ With remainder

Date: ....

Name: ....

Score: ...... /16

1) 6)742

R

2) 6)829

R

3) 3)980

R

4) 4)787

R

5) 3)753

R

6) 5)829

R

7) 3)875

R

8) 3)725

R

9) 3)977

R

10) 6)974

R

11) 6)938

R

12) 5)725

R

13) 3)821

R

14) 3)973

R

15) 3)812

R

16) 6)994

R

♪ Long Division

★ Level 2
★ 3-Digit dividends
★ With remainder

Date: ....

Name: ....

Score: ...... /16

☆1	☆2	☆3	☆4
6)704	3)875	6)881	3)786
R	R	R	R

☆5	☆6	☆7	☆8
5)932	2)902	2)904	2)843
R	R	R	R

☆9	☆10	☆11	☆12
4)712	2)989	3)886	4)978
R	R	R	R

☆13	☆14	☆15	☆16
2)917	2)704	4)728	4)944
R	R	R	R

Long Division
★ Level 2
★ 3-Digit dividends
★ With remainder

Date: ....

Name: ....

Score: ...... /16

1. $7 \overline{)709}$ R

2. $4 \overline{)875}$ R

3. $7 \overline{)706}$ R

4. $3 \overline{)756}$ R

5. $3 \overline{)978}$ R

6. $6 \overline{)779}$ R

7. $3 \overline{)887}$ R

8. $3 \overline{)863}$ R

9. $3 \overline{)973}$ R

10. $3 \overline{)909}$ R

11. $7 \overline{)749}$ R

12. $2 \overline{)963}$ R

13. $3 \overline{)812}$ R

14. $6 \overline{)815}$ R

15. $3 \overline{)760}$ R

16. $2 \overline{)916}$ R

Long Division

★ Level 2
★ 3-Digit dividends
★ With remainder

Date: ....

Name: ....

Score: ...... /16

1	2	3	4
6)877	4)743	4)930	6)882

5	6	7	8
5)843	4)807	5)877	5)876

9	10	11	12
6)822	4)703	6)776	6)898

13	14	15	16
3)956	2)754	4)902	5)924

)Long Division

★ Level 2
★ 3-Digit dividends
★ With remainder

1   4)793   R

2   7)924   R

3   5)913   R

4   4)937   R

5   3)795   R

6   7)935   R

7   5)838   R

8   6)718   R

9   6)798   R

10   7)981   R

11   2)983   R

12   6)889   R

13   5)942   R

14   7)786   R

15   4)896   R

16   3)920   R

Long Division

★ Level 2
★ 3-Digit dividends
★ With remainder

Date: ....

Name: ....

Score: ...... /16

① 2)444

― ↓

― ↓

―

R

② 2)642

― ↓

― ↓

―

R

③ 4)657

― ↓

― ↓

―

R

④ 3)461

― ↓

― ↓

―

R

⑤ 4)521

― ↓

― ↓

―

R

⑥ 3)736

― ↓

― ↓

―

R

⑦ 3)693

― ↓

― ↓

―

R

⑧ 3)602

― ↓

― ↓

―

R

⑨ 3)550

― ↓

― ↓

―

R

⑩ 3)727

― ↓

― ↓

―

R

⑪ 4)472

― ↓

― ↓

―

R

⑫ 4)459

― ↓

― ↓

―

R

⑬ 3)647

― ↓

― ↓

―

R

⑭ 4)523

― ↓

― ↓

―

R

⑮ 3)643

― ↓

― ↓

―

R

⑯ 4)683

― ↓

― ↓

―

R

Date: ....

Name: ....

Score: ...... /16

1	2	3	4
2)4 8 6	3)5 7 5	4)5 0 9	3)4 7 6

5	6	7	8
4)7 4 6	2)5 1 7	3)5 1 8	4)7 6 1

9	10	11	12
3)7 3 9	3)4 5 4	2)4 1 6	4)6 7 4

13	14	15	16
2)4 2 3	3)6 5 0	3)4 0 9	3)6 8 2

Long Division

★ Level 2
★ 3-Digit dividends
★ With remainder

Date: ....

Name: ....

Score: ...... /16

1 3)706 R

2 3)525 R

3 3)511 R

4 3)426 R

5 2)645 R

6 2)466 R

7 3)541 R

8 3)590 R

9 3)703 R

10 3)785 R

11 2)410 R

12 3)667 R

13 3)465 R

14 3)664 R

15 3)665 R

16 4)792 R

Long Division

★ Level 2
★ 3-Digit dividends
★ With remainder

Date: ....

Name: ....

Score: ...... /16

1) 2)559 R

2) 4)734 R

3) 3)670 R

4) 3)677 R

5) 3)541 R

6) 3)649 R

7) 3)640 R

8) 4)795 R

9) 2)577 R

10) 3)441 R

11) 2)509 R

12) 2)775 R

13) 4)407 R

14) 2)714 R

15) 3)416 R

16) 3)463 R

@MathematicsByKim

-41-

Long Division
★ Level 2
★ 3-Digit dividends
★ With remainder

Date: ....

Name: ....

Score: ...... /16

1. 5) 7 1 5 — R

2. 5) 9 0 3 — R

3. 5) 7 2 3 — R

4. 6) 7 0 8 — R

5. 5) 7 7 5 — R

6. 7) 7 0 6 — R

7. 6) 8 7 6 — R

8. 6) 9 9 8 — R

9. 7) 8 0 9 — R

10. 7) 7 1 2 — R

11. 5) 8 9 6 — R

12. 6) 9 7 0 — R

13. 7) 9 4 2 — R

14. 6) 9 8 5 — R

15. 6) 7 7 9 — R

16. 6) 9 2 3 — R

♪ Long Division
★ Level 2
★ 3-Digit dividends
★ With remainder

Date: ....

Name: ....

Score: ...... /16

1 8) 8 0 4   R

2 8) 9 2 5   R

3 8) 8 6 9   R

4 6) 8 8 1   R

5 7) 9 7 1   R

6 6) 9 0 1   R

7 6) 8 9 3   R

8 6) 8 9 9   R

9 7) 9 9 0   R

10 7) 8 1 0   R

11 8) 8 6 4   R

12 8) 9 7 4   R

13 8) 9 7 1   R

14 7) 9 0 1   R

15 6) 8 5 2   R

16 7) 9 8 3   R

♪ Long Division
★ Level 2
★ 3-Digit dividends
★ With remainder

Date: ....

Name: ....

Score: ...... /16

1 $7\overline{)973}$ R

2 $9\overline{)931}$ R

3 $8\overline{)971}$ R

4 $8\overline{)944}$ R

5 $8\overline{)959}$ R

6 $8\overline{)998}$ R

7 $7\overline{)902}$ R

8 $9\overline{)938}$ R

9 $9\overline{)918}$ R

10 $9\overline{)905}$ R

11 $8\overline{)991}$ R

12 $8\overline{)990}$ R

13 $9\overline{)996}$ R

14 $7\overline{)970}$ R

15 $7\overline{)982}$ R

16 $9\overline{)967}$ R

) Long Division

★ Level 3
★ 4-Digit dividends
★ No remainder

Date: ....

Name: ....

Score: ...... /16

---

1   6) 8 9 1 0   R

2   6) 8 5 4 4   R

3   2) 8 0 1 8   R

4   2) 8 0 6 8   R

5   7) 8 4 3 5   R

6   2) 9 2 9 8   R

7   3) 9 9 5 7   R

8   7) 8 7 2 2   R

9   4) 7 4 4 0   R

10   5) 9 9 4 5   R

11   4) 7 5 3 6   R

12   3) 7 4 2 8   R

13   5) 8 1 1 0   R

14   5) 9 7 7 0   R

15   3) 7 0 1 4   R

16   6) 7 9 0 8   R

@MathematicsByKim

-45-

) Long Division
★ Level 3
★ 4-Digit dividends
★ No remainder

Date: ....

Name: ....

Score: ...... /16

1 $2\overline{)8352}$ R

2 $6\overline{)8016}$ R

3 $3\overline{)7716}$ R

4 $2\overline{)7880}$ R

5 $5\overline{)8545}$ R

6 $5\overline{)7640}$ R

7 $2\overline{)8566}$ R

8 $3\overline{)9021}$ R

9 $7\overline{)7938}$ R

10 $3\overline{)9294}$ R

11 $7\overline{)9443}$ R

12 $7\overline{)9506}$ R

13 $6\overline{)8508}$ R

14 $6\overline{)8844}$ R

15 $7\overline{)8757}$ R

16 $3\overline{)9027}$ R

) Long Division

★ Level 3
★ 4-Digit dividends
★ No remainder

Date: ....

Name: ....

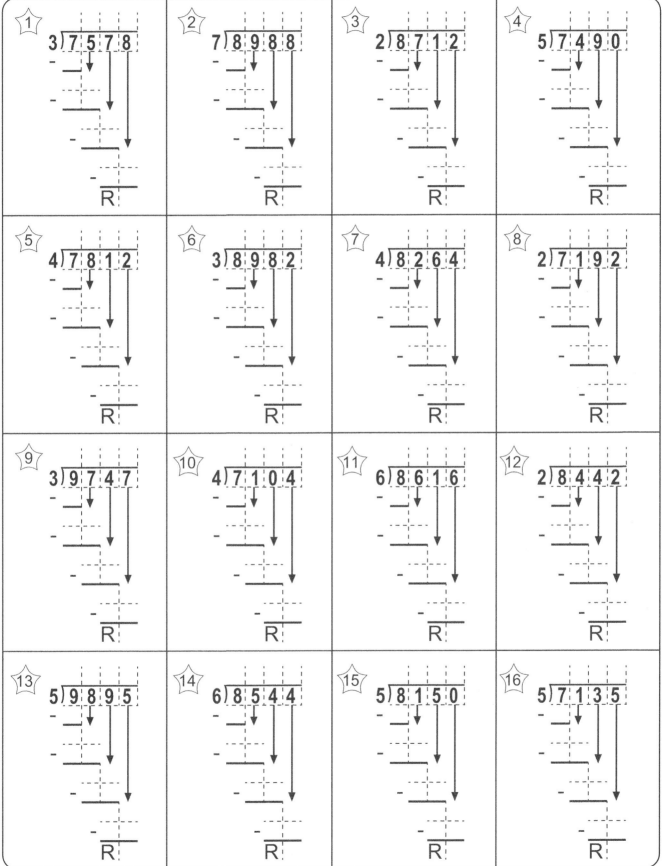

1. 3) 7 5 7 8   R
2. 7) 8 9 8 8   R
3. 2) 8 7 1 2   R
4. 5) 7 4 9 0   R

5. 4) 7 8 1 2   R
6. 3) 8 9 8 2   R
7. 4) 8 2 6 4   R
8. 2) 7 1 9 2   R

9. 3) 9 7 4 7   R
10. 4) 7 1 0 4   R
11. 6) 8 6 1 6   R
12. 2) 8 4 4 2   R

13. 5) 9 8 9 5   R
14. 6) 8 5 4 4   R
15. 5) 8 1 5 0   R
16. 5) 7 1 3 5   R

Long Division

★ Level 3
★ 4-Digit dividends
★ No remainder

Date: ....

Name: ....

Score: ...... /16

1	2	3	4
7) 7 7 2 1	3) 7 7 9 7	2) 7 1 0 2	3) 7 3 6 2

5	6	7	8
6) 9 9 2 4	4) 9 6 4 0	7) 7 2 9 4	4) 7 2 0 4

9	10	11	12
3) 8 5 2 3	6) 7 5 6 0	4) 9 5 5 6	2) 9 4 1 2

13	14	15	16
3) 8 8 0 2	7) 9 9 4 0	5) 7 1 9 0	5) 7 4 9 0

)Long Division

★ Level 3
★ 4-Digit dividends
★ No remainder

Date: ....

Name: ....

Score: ...... /16

1	6) 9 6 4 8	R

2	7) 8 5 7 5	R

3	6) 8 8 0 8	R

4	5) 7 1 9 0	R

5	3) 9 9 5 4	R

6	5) 8 0 5 5	R

7	6) 9 8 1 6	R

8	3) 8 0 2 2	R

9	2) 9 6 6 2	R

10	7) 7 1 8 9	R

11	2) 9 5 0 0	R

12	4) 7 4 0 8	R

13	4) 9 2 0 0	R

14	6) 7 1 8 8	R

15	6) 8 5 8 6	R

16	7) 7 7 4 9	R

Long Division

★ Level 3
★ 4-Digit dividends
★ No remainder

Date: ....

Name: ....

Score: ...... /16

1) 6) 7 4 9 4   R

2) 6) 9 4 9 8   R

3) 2) 9 4 3 4   R

4) 3) 8 6 7 3   R

5) 4) 9 0 3 6   R

6) 4) 7 2 6 4   R

7) 6) 8 9 0 4   R

8) 5) 9 1 2 5   R

9) 2) 7 3 2 4   R

10) 6) 7 3 8 6   R

11) 5) 8 4 3 5   R

12) 7) 9 5 5 5   R

13) 3) 8 4 1 8   R

14) 3) 8 3 6 4   R

15) 3) 8 5 0 2   R

16) 4) 7 2 5 6   R

Long Division

★ Level 3
★ 4-Digit dividends
★ No remainder

Date: ....

Name: ....

Score: ...... /16

1 $3 \overline{)8\,0\,6\,7}$ R	**2** $2 \overline{)7\,2\,2\,4}$ R	**3** $3 \overline{)7\,1\,9\,7}$ R	**4** $4 \overline{)9\,4\,4\,4}$ R
5 $4 \overline{)7\,9\,4\,4}$ R	**6** $3 \overline{)9\,1\,5\,3}$ R	**7** $6 \overline{)9\,6\,6\,6}$ R	**8** $5 \overline{)9\,9\,4\,5}$ R
9 $7 \overline{)8\,5\,0\,5}$ R	**10** $6 \overline{)8\,6\,2\,8}$ R	**11** $7 \overline{)9\,5\,3\,4}$ R	**12** $5 \overline{)9\,1\,0\,5}$ R
13 $2 \overline{)7\,5\,4\,6}$ R	**14** $5 \overline{)8\,5\,5\,0}$ R	**15** $3 \overline{)7\,4\,1\,6}$ R	**16** $4 \overline{)8\,6\,3\,6}$ R

♪ Long Division

★ Level 3
★ 4-Digit dividends
★ No remainder

Date: ....

Name: ....

Score: ...... /16

1	2	3	4
5) 8 5 6 5	5) 7 2 0 0	5) 9 4 9 5	5) 7 1 7 0

5	6	7	8
7) 9 8 0 0	4) 9 5 9 6	6) 8 5 5 6	5) 7 7 4 0

9	10	11	12
4) 8 8 2 8	2) 7 2 4 4	6) 7 7 6 4	6) 9 3 4 2

13	14	15	16
4) 8 1 1 6	3) 7 9 2 0	6) 8 8 7 4	3) 9 3 7 5

@MathematicsByKim

-52-

Long Division

★ Level 3
★ 4-Digit dividends
★ No remainder

Date: ....

Name: ....

Score: ...... /16

1	2	3	4
3) 7 3 7 1	3) 9 9 8 4	6) 8 6 9 4	4) 8 4 8 4

5	6	7	8
7) 9 9 6 8	5) 9 6 0 0	5) 7 2 1 5	2) 8 5 8 4

9	10	11	12
6) 8 6 4 6	4) 9 6 0 0	4) 8 3 8 0	4) 9 5 1 6

13	14	15	16
3) 8 8 2 0	2) 7 6 5 4	5) 8 1 1 0	6) 9 0 4 2

@MathematicsByKim

-53-

Long Division
★ Level 3
★ 4-Digit dividends
★ No remainder

Date: ....

Name: ....

Score: ...... /16

1) $7\overline{)7525}$ R

2) $4\overline{)7556}$ R

3) $5\overline{)7580}$ R

4) $3\overline{)9297}$ R

5) $4\overline{)7840}$ R

6) $5\overline{)8160}$ R

7) $3\overline{)9837}$ R

8) $2\overline{)8752}$ R

9) $3\overline{)9168}$ R

10) $4\overline{)7852}$ R

11) $7\overline{)7819}$ R

12) $2\overline{)8680}$ R

13) $6\overline{)7974}$ R

14) $6\overline{)8352}$ R

15) $5\overline{)8930}$ R

16) $5\overline{)9690}$ R

Long Division

★ Level 3
★ 4-Digit dividends
★ No remainder

Date: ....

Name: ....

Score: ...... /16

1	2	3	4
3) 7 6 6 5	4) 7 2 2 4	2) 5 0 9 6	3) 5 3 1 0

5	6	7	8
2) 6 5 7 2	4) 5 2 0 8	4) 6 1 0 0	4) 5 4 8 0

9	10	11	12
4) 6 9 8 0	3) 4 9 4 4	4) 5 8 0 8	3) 7 8 0 9

13	14	15	16
4) 5 7 6 0	3) 6 8 1 3	3) 7 7 2 5	2) 6 0 7 0

)Long Division
★ Level 3
★ 4-Digit dividends
★ No remainder

Date: ....

Name: ....

Score: ...... /16

1   2)5 2 8 0
    R

2   3)6 3 8 4
    R

3   2)4 2 7 4
    R

4   3)4 0 4 4
    R

5   2)7 1 3 8
    R

6   4)7 2 4 8
    R

7   3)5 4 7 8
    R

8   3)6 5 5 5
    R

9   3)7 7 3 4
    R

10 2)5 1 7 0
    R

11 3)7 3 9 2
    R

12 2)4 4 7 6
    R

13 3)6 4 7 7
    R

14 3)6 4 5 6
    R

15 4)5 2 5 2
    R

16 4)6 0 5 6
    R

Long Division

★ Level 3
★ 4-Digit dividends
★ No remainder

Date: ....

Name: ....

Score: ...... /16

1   2)7378   R

2   3)4155   R

3   3)6576   R

4   3)5040   R

5   3)6801   R

6   3)6312   R

7   3)6882   R

8   2)4866   R

9   3)6846   R

10   2)6696   R

11   3)4326   R

12   3)5955   R

13   3)4215   R

14   2)6812   R

15   3)7854   R

16   2)7412   R

Long Division

★ Level 3
★ 4-Digit dividends
★ No remainder

Date: ....

Name: ....

Score: ...... /16

① $3\overline{)6939}$	② $2\overline{)5474}$	③ $3\overline{)5598}$	④ $4\overline{)7812}$
⑤ $3\overline{)5883}$	⑥ $3\overline{)6900}$	⑦ $2\overline{)5210}$	⑧ $4\overline{)5260}$
⑨ $4\overline{)7112}$	⑩ $3\overline{)7122}$	⑪ $3\overline{)7149}$	⑫ $3\overline{)6696}$
⑬ $3\overline{)5451}$	⑭ $3\overline{)7407}$	⑮ $3\overline{)6024}$	⑯ $3\overline{)7188}$

Long Division

★ Level 3
★ 4-Digit dividends
★ No remainder

Date: ....

Name: ....

Score: ...... /16

① 6)8898	② 7)9821	③ 6)7008	④ 7)9807
R	R	R	R

⑤ 7)9569	⑥ 6)8610	⑦ 7)8148	⑧ 7)8722
R	R	R	R

⑨ 7)8162	⑩ 7)7672	⑪ 7)8645	⑫ 6)9054
R	R	R	R

⑬ 6)8040	⑭ 6)8268	⑮ 7)8505	⑯ 7)8428
R	R	R	R

Long Division

★ Level 3
★ 4-Digit dividends
★ No remainder

Date: ....

Name: ....

Score: ...... /16

1   7) 9 9 2 6   R

2   8) 8 0 0 0   R

3   8) 8 5 7 6   R

4   8) 8 0 4 0   R

5   7) 8 8 7 6   R

6   7) 9 6 4 6   R

7   8) 9 8 3 2   R

8   7) 8 5 4 7   R

9   8) 9 1 1 2   R

10   8) 8 4 8 0   R

11   7) 9 9 7 5   R

12   7) 8 2 1 1   R

13   8) 9 5 1 2   R

14   8) 9 8 8 0   R

15   8) 9 7 6 0   R

16   8) 9 1 9 2   R

Long Division
★ Level 3
★ 4-Digit dividends
★ No remainder

Date: ....

Name: ....

Score: ...... /16

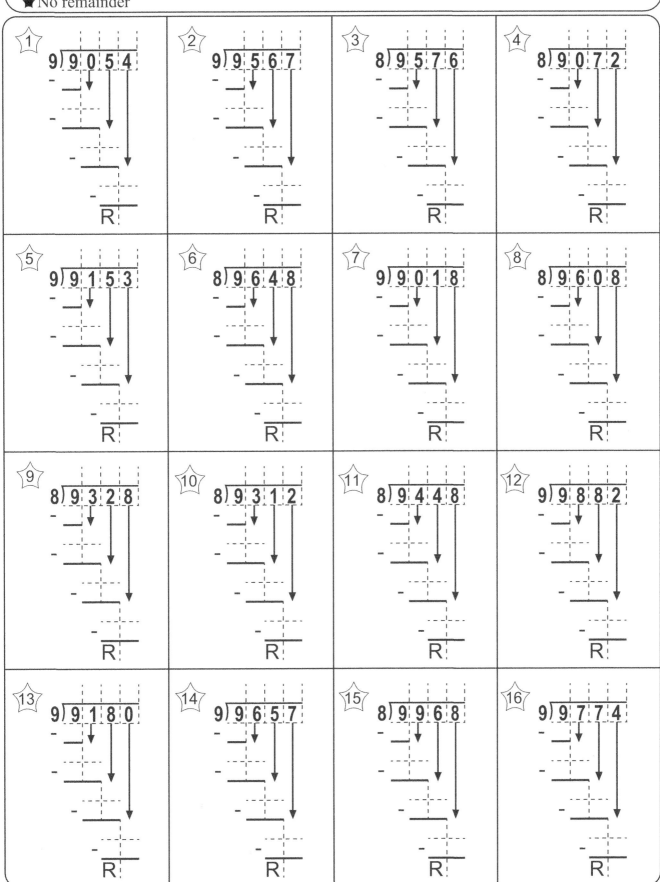

1. $9\overline{)9054}$

2. $9\overline{)9567}$

3. $8\overline{)9576}$

4. $8\overline{)9072}$

5. $9\overline{)9153}$

6. $8\overline{)9648}$

7. $9\overline{)9018}$

8. $8\overline{)9608}$

9. $8\overline{)9328}$

10. $8\overline{)9312}$

11. $8\overline{)9448}$

12. $9\overline{)9882}$

13. $9\overline{)9180}$

14. $9\overline{)9657}$

15. $8\overline{)9968}$

16. $9\overline{)9774}$

♩Long Division

★ Level 4
★ 4-Digit dividends
★ With remainder

Date: ....

Name: ....

Score: ...... /16

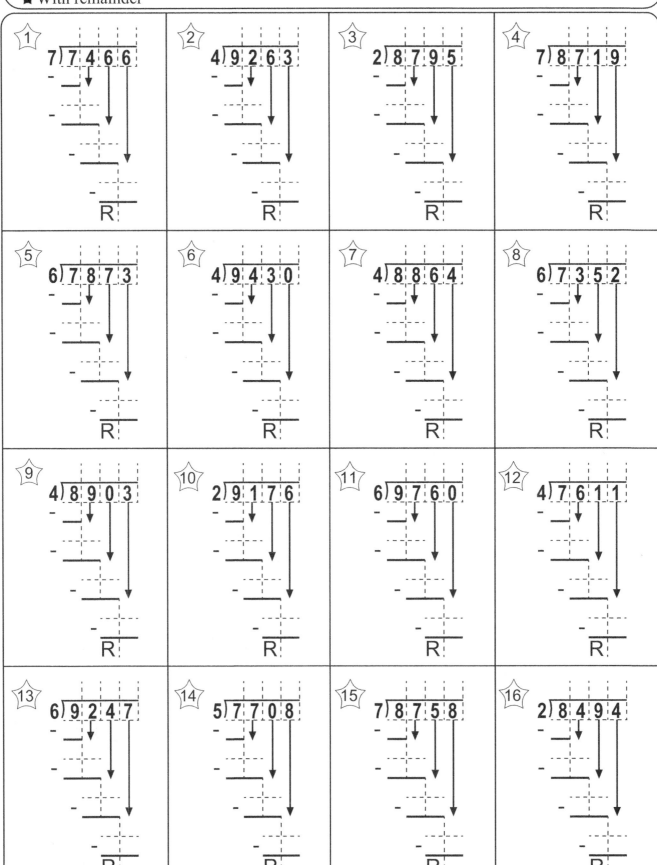

1. 7⟌7 4 6 6   R

2. 4⟌9 2 6 3   R

3. 2⟌8 7 9 5   R

4. 7⟌8 7 1 9   R

5. 6⟌7 8 7 3   R

6. 4⟌9 4 3 0   R

7. 4⟌8 8 6 4   R

8. 6⟌7 3 5 2   R

9. 4⟌8 9 0 3   R

10. 2⟌9 1 7 6   R

11. 6⟌9 7 6 0   R

12. 4⟌7 6 1 1   R

13. 6⟌9 2 4 7   R

14. 5⟌7 7 0 8   R

15. 7⟌8 7 5 8   R

16. 2⟌8 4 9 4   R

Long Division

★ Level 4
★ 4-Digit dividends
★ With remainder

Date: ....

Name: ....

Score: ...... /16

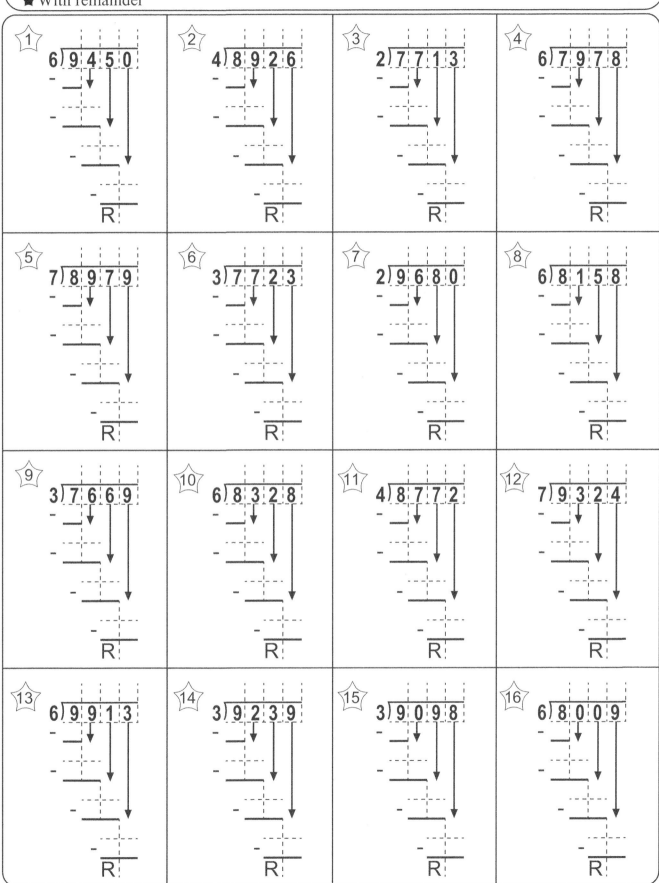

Long Division
★ Level 4
★ 4-Digit dividends
★ With remainder

Date: ....

Name: ....

Score: ...... /16

1	2	3	4
5)7184	2)9015	6)8584	4)9427
5	6	7	8
5)9558	5)7963	5)7010	5)7601
9	10	11	12
2)8618	5)9624	4)9414	7)9949
13	14	15	16
2)9263	7)9597	4)7934	2)9834

♪ Long Division
★ Level 4
★ 4-Digit dividends
★ With remainder

Date: ....

Name: ....

Score: ...... /16

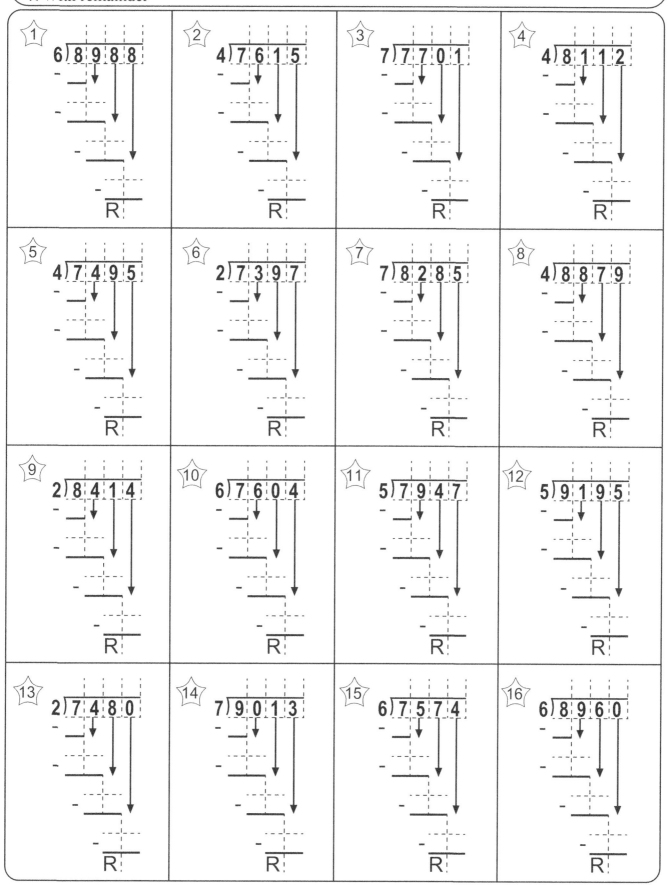

1) 6) 8 9 8 8   R

2) 4) 7 6 1 5   R

3) 7) 7 7 0 1   R

4) 4) 8 1 1 2   R

5) 4) 7 4 9 5   R

6) 2) 7 3 9 7   R

7) 7) 8 2 8 5   R

8) 4) 8 8 7 9   R

9) 2) 8 4 1 4   R

10) 6) 7 6 0 4   R

11) 5) 7 9 4 7   R

12) 5) 9 1 9 5   R

13) 2) 7 4 8 0   R

14) 7) 9 0 1 3   R

15) 6) 7 5 7 4   R

16) 6) 8 9 6 0   R

Long Division

★ Level 4
★ 4-Digit dividends
★ With remainder

Date: ....

Name: ....

Score: ...... /16

1) 6) 9 2 1 6
R

2) 5) 8 0 2 4
R

3) 4) 7 4 6 1
R

4) 3) 7 6 3 3
R

5) 5) 8 7 3 2
R

6) 5) 7 3 8 8
R

7) 5) 8 7 7 6
R

8) 5) 8 0 2 1
R

9) 6) 9 5 8 4
R

10) 2) 8 4 3 4
R

11) 2) 9 9 2 4
R

12) 4) 9 5 4 0
R

13) 4) 8 2 6 3
R

14) 2) 7 2 1 4
R

15) 2) 8 3 8 5
R

16) 5) 9 4 4 0
R

Long Division
★ Level 4
★ 4-Digit dividends
★ With remainder

Date: ....

Name: ....

Score: ...... /16

1) 3)̅8̅ ̅3̅ ̅8̅ ̅2̅   R

2) 6)̅9̅ ̅6̅ ̅7̅ ̅9̅   R

3) 2)̅7̅ ̅6̅ ̅6̅ ̅6̅   R

4) 4)̅9̅ ̅9̅ ̅5̅ ̅8̅   R

5) 4)̅9̅ ̅1̅ ̅7̅ ̅6̅   R

6) 7)̅7̅ ̅9̅ ̅5̅ ̅0̅   R

7) 3)̅8̅ ̅5̅ ̅2̅ ̅4̅   R

8) 4)̅8̅ ̅1̅ ̅2̅ ̅3̅   R

9) 4)̅8̅ ̅7̅ ̅8̅ ̅4̅   R

10) 7)̅7̅ ̅4̅ ̅8̅ ̅2̅   R

11) 4)̅9̅ ̅2̅ ̅7̅ ̅7̅   R

12) 3)̅9̅ ̅4̅ ̅6̅ ̅1̅   R

13) 3)̅9̅ ̅3̅ ̅3̅ ̅3̅   R

14) 6)̅8̅ ̅8̅ ̅1̅ ̅0̅   R

15) 6)̅9̅ ̅1̅ ̅1̅ ̅2̅   R

16) 5)̅8̅ ̅0̅ ̅6̅ ̅1̅   R

) Long Division
★ Level 4
★ 4-Digit dividends
★ With remainder

Date: ....

Name: ....

Score: ...... /16

1 6) 9 7 7 3   R

2 6) 7 8 8 4   R

3 3) 8 9 3 6   R

4 4) 9 2 5 0   R

5 4) 9 8 4 1   R

6 5) 9 2 5 9   R

7 4) 9 0 2 7   R

8 4) 7 1 4 0   R

9 3) 8 7 3 0   R

10 3) 8 0 0 4   R

11 6) 7 2 7 5   R

12 6) 8 3 5 7   R

13 7) 7 2 2 2   R

14 5) 8 7 2 7   R

15 3) 7 2 7 4   R

16 2) 7 8 5 2   R

) Long Division
★ Level 4
★ 4-Digit dividends
★ With remainder

Date: ....

Name: ....

Score: ...... /16

1. $5 \overline{) 7\ 8\ 7\ 4}$ R

2. $3 \overline{) 8\ 2\ 1\ 2}$ R

3. $7 \overline{) 9\ 0\ 8\ 7}$ R

4. $5 \overline{) 9\ 4\ 6\ 7}$ R

5. $4 \overline{) 9\ 9\ 5\ 5}$ R

6. $6 \overline{) 9\ 1\ 4\ 0}$ R

7. $7 \overline{) 7\ 3\ 7\ 1}$ R

8. $5 \overline{) 7\ 2\ 5\ 8}$ R

9. $5 \overline{) 7\ 4\ 9\ 3}$ R

10. $2 \overline{) 9\ 9\ 6\ 4}$ R

11. $6 \overline{) 8\ 1\ 9\ 1}$ R

12. $4 \overline{) 8\ 2\ 1\ 6}$ R

13. $5 \overline{) 7\ 4\ 9\ 6}$ R

14. $4 \overline{) 9\ 7\ 9\ 9}$ R

15. $5 \overline{) 7\ 9\ 7\ 9}$ R

16. $5 \overline{) 7\ 8\ 4\ 3}$ R

) Long Division

★ Level 4
★ 4-Digit dividends
★ With remainder

Date: ....

Name: ....

Score: ...... /16

1

$6 \overline{)7563}$

R

2

$2 \overline{)8738}$

R

3

$5 \overline{)8862}$

R

4

$3 \overline{)7282}$

R

5

$4 \overline{)9159}$

R

6

$6 \overline{)8497}$

R

7

$2 \overline{)9306}$

R

8

$2 \overline{)9676}$

R

9

$5 \overline{)7016}$

R

10

$3 \overline{)8427}$

R

11

$5 \overline{)8620}$

R

12

$2 \overline{)8178}$

R

13

$6 \overline{)7049}$

R

14

$6 \overline{)7097}$

R

15

$5 \overline{)7525}$

R

16

$4 \overline{)9391}$

R

Long Division

★ Level 4
★ 4-Digit dividends
★ With remainder

Date: ....

Name: ....

Score: ...... /16

1	5) 8 3 3 7
2	7) 3 3 7 6
3	3) 9 0 9 0
4	6) 7 9 1 9

R

5	4) 9 5 3 9
6	2) 7 7 7 1
7	7) 8 2 5 8
8	6) 7 1 5 3

R

9	3) 8 4 0 2
10	4) 7 1 6 2
11	5) 9 7 8 0
12	5) 9 9 8 5

R

13	4) 8 4 2 8
14	7) 9 1 0 4
15	4) 8 7 7 5
16	6) 8 2 0 7

R

Long Division

★ Level 4
★ 4-Digit dividends
★ With remainder

Date: ....

Name: ....

Score: ...... /16

1) 4) 5 2 4 4   R

2) 2) 4 3 7 4   R

3) 2) 7 5 0 6   R

4) 3) 4 6 7 8   R

5) 4) 6 9 4 9   R

6) 2) 6 0 4 2   R

7) 2) 7 2 9 4   R

8) 2) 4 2 8 4   R

9) 2) 6 9 3 5   R

10) 3) 7 1 1 4   R

11) 4) 6 9 1 6   R

12) 4) 5 7 2 7   R

13) 3) 5 8 2 3   R

14) 4) 4 2 8 7   R

15) 3) 6 8 4 3   R

16) 4) 5 6 2 0   R

⟩Long Division
★ Level 4
★ 4-Digit dividends
★ With remainder

Date: ....

Name: ....

Score: ...... /16

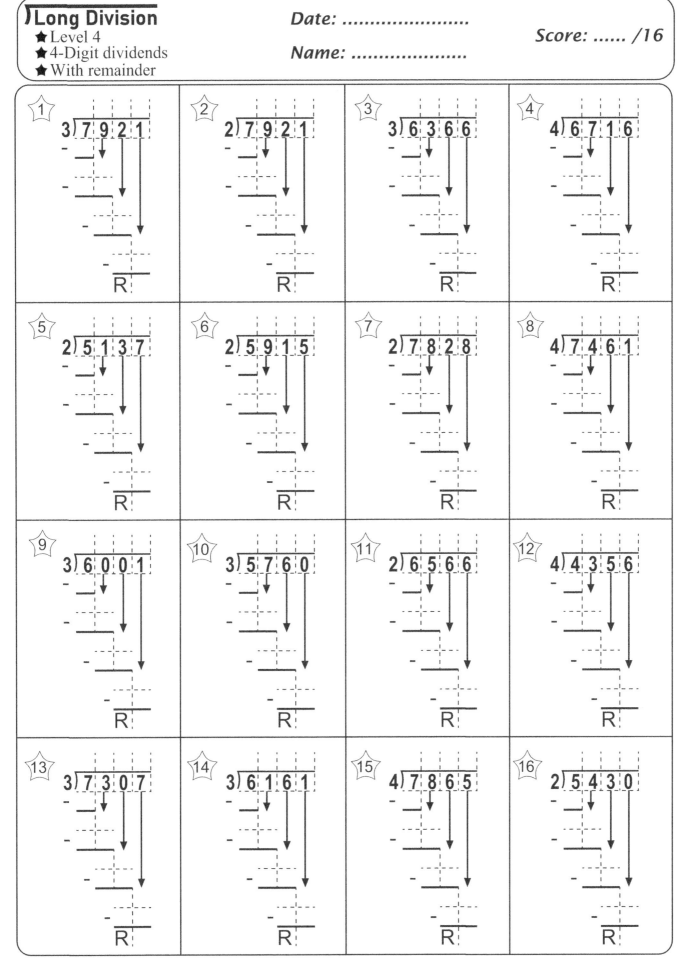

1. 3⟌7 9 2 1

2. 2⟌7 9 2 1

3. 3⟌6 3 6 6

4. 4⟌6 7 1 6

5. 2⟌5 1 3 7

6. 2⟌5 9 1 5

7. 2⟌7 8 2 8

8. 4⟌7 4 6 1

9. 3⟌6 0 0 1

10. 3⟌5 7 6 0

11. 2⟌6 5 6 6

12. 4⟌4 3 5 6

13. 3⟌7 3 0 7

14. 3⟌6 1 6 1

15. 4⟌7 8 6 5

16. 2⟌5 4 3 0

⌐ Long Division

★ Level 4
★ 4-Digit dividends
★ With remainder

Date: ....

Name: ....

Score: ...... /16

☆1	☆2	☆3	☆4
2) 5 0 6 4	2) 5 8 7 9	2) 6 2 5 1	3) 5 4 7 8
R	R	R	R

☆5	☆6	☆7	☆8
3) 7 0 5 0	4) 4 7 5 4	3) 7 3 4 8	3) 5 3 8 1
R	R	R	R

☆9	☆10	☆11	☆12
2) 6 5 8 2	4) 5 0 8 7	4) 5 3 9 0	3) 6 1 8 2
R	R	R	R

☆13	☆14	☆15	☆16
2) 5 1 8 1	2) 6 0 2 0	3) 4 7 3 4	3) 4 5 1 1
R	R	R	R

@MathematicsByKim

-74-

♩ Long Division
★ Level 4
★ 4-Digit dividends
★ With remainder

Date: ....

Name: ....

Score: ...... /16

1) $2\overline{)5783}$ R

2) $3\overline{)7460}$ R

3) $2\overline{)6761}$ R

4) $3\overline{)6949}$ R

5) $4\overline{)5056}$ R

6) $3\overline{)5813}$ R

7) $3\overline{)6290}$ R

8) $3\overline{)7750}$ R

9) $4\overline{)4274}$ R

10) $3\overline{)6816}$ R

11) $3\overline{)4599}$ R

12) $4\overline{)5899}$ R

13) $4\overline{)6632}$ R

14) $4\overline{)4686}$ R

15) $4\overline{)4669}$ R

16) $2\overline{)7149}$ R

Long Division

★ Level 4
★ 4-Digit dividends
★ With remainder

Date: ....

Name: ....

Score: ...... /16

1) 7) 8 2 0 5
   R

2) 7) 9 8 3 9
   R

3) 6) 9 2 9 3
   R

4) 7) 9 0 9 5
   R

5) 6) 8 7 5 1
   R

6) 7) 9 9 3 5
   R

7) 6) 8 3 2 8
   R

8) 7) 7 6 9 3
   R

9) 7) 9 2 1 5
   R

10) 6) 7 1 5 6
    R

11) 6) 9 8 6 0
    R

12) 6) 9 8 0 1
    R

13) 6) 8 7 1 8
    R

14) 6) 9 6 3 1
    R

15) 6) 7 2 3 3
    R

16) 7) 8 2 1 5
    R

Long Division

★ Level 4
★ 4-Digit dividends
★ With remainder

Date: ....

Name: ....

1) 8) 8 6 1 5   R

2) 8) 9 3 2 1   R

3) 7) 9 4 0 3   R

4) 8) 9 2 2 1   R

5) 8) 9 3 6 1   R

6) 8) 8 9 1 1   R

7) 8) 8 1 6 6   R

8) 8) 8 7 7 9   R

9) 8) 8 7 8 7   R

10) 8) 9 2 9 6   R

11) 8) 9 8 7 6   R

12) 7) 9 5 8 7   R

13) 7) 9 6 5 7   R

14) 8) 8 9 7 2   R

15) 7) 9 3 5 7   R

16) 7) 9 1 6 7   R

Long Division

★ Level 4
★ 4-Digit dividends
★ With remainder

Date: ....

Name: ....

Score: ...... /16

1 9)9653

R

2 9)9021

R

3 8)9936

R

4 8)9620

R

5 8)9069

R

6 9)9119

R

7 8)9248

R

8 9)9899

R

9 8)9170

R

10 8)9299

R

11 9)9179

R

12 8)9871

R

13 9)9498

R

14 9)9778

R

15 9)9134

R

16 9)9662

R

Long Division
★ Challenge yourself
★ 2-Digit dividends
★ 2-Digit divisors

Date: ....

Name: ....

Score: ...... /16

1. 51)9180

2. 22)8162

3. 66)7986

4. 46)8050

5. 66)9504

6. 41)7913

7. 63)7434

8. 30)7380

9. 20)9300

10. 52)8112

11. 37)9546

12. 55)8470

13. 21)8694

14. 32)9664

15. 58)8062

16. 60)7140

Long Division

★ Challenge yourself
★ 2-Digit dividends
★ 2-Digit divisors

Date: ....

Name: ....

Score: ...... /16

⭐1 69)7 3 8 3
          R

⭐2 29)9 0 1 9
          R

⭐3 40)7 5 2 0
          R

⭐4 34)9 2 8 2
          R

⭐5 23)7 8 4 3
          R

⭐6 37)7 6 5 9
          R

⭐7 36)7 8 1 2
          R

⭐8 33)8 7 7 8
          R

⭐9 60)7 2 6 0
          R

⭐10 70)8 4 0 0
          R

⭐11 51)9 2 8 2
          R

⭐12 50)7 0 5 0
          R

⭐13 40)8 3 6 0
          R

⭐14 36)7 7 4 0
          R

⭐15 33)7 1 9 4
          R

⭐16 31)7 1 3 0
          R

)Long Division

Date: ....

Name: ....

Score: ...... /16

① 51)8 2 1 1

② 43)8 9 4 4

③ 62)9 7 9 6

④ 49)7 4 9 7

⑤ 43)8 6 0 0

⑥ 43)7 1 3 8

⑦ 61)8 7 8 4

⑧ 20)9 7 4 0

⑨ 36)7 9 2 0

⑩ 40)8 1 6 0

⑪ 25)9 2 0 0

⑫ 56)7 5 6 0

⑬ 31)7 7 8 1

⑭ 55)6 9 8 5

⑮ 27)9 2 0 7

⑯ 23)8 5 7 9

@MathematicsByKim

Long Division

★ Challenge yourself
★ 2-Digit dividends
★ 2-Digit divisors

Date: ....

Name: ....

Score: ...... /16

1) 22)7326

R

2) 21)7497

R

3) 58)7540

R

4) 28)7924

R

5) 41)9717

R

6) 67)9313

R

7) 50)7750

R

8) 41)9225

R

9) 64)7936

R

10) 44)7348

R

11) 52)7644

R

12) 26)9672

R

13) 69)8694

R

14) 40)7440

R

15) 27)8937

R

16) 35)8470

R

)Long Division
★ Challenge yourself
★ 2-Digit dividends
★ 2-Digit divisors

Date: ....

Name: ....

Score: ...... /16

1 41)9 5 5 3

2 61)9 5 1 6

3 53)7 0 4 9

4 20)9 6 4 0

5 29)9 6 5 7

6 67)7 8 3 9

7 46)7 6 3 6

8 22)9 0 2 0

9 37)8 9 5 4

10 56)8 6 2 4

11 23)9 2 9 2

12 35)9 4 5 0

13 51)7 2 9 3

14 53)9 1 6 9

15 57)7 6 3 8

16 34)9 6 9 0

♪ Long Division

★ Challenge yourself
★ 2-Digit dividends
★ 2-Digit divisors

Date: ....

Name: ....

Score: ...... /16

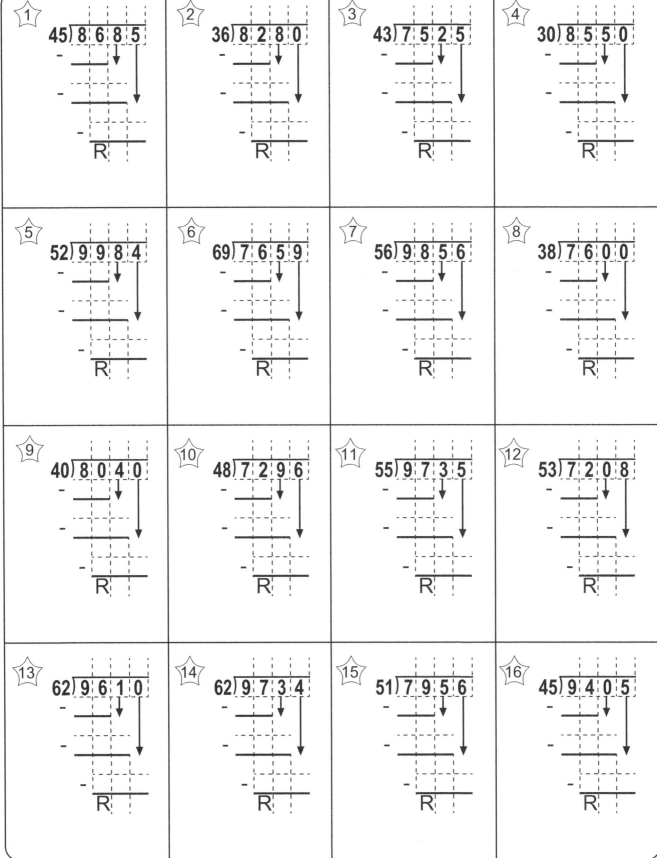

1 45)8 6 8 5

2 36)8 2 8 0

3 43)7 5 2 5

4 30)8 5 5 0

5 52)9 9 8 4

6 69)7 6 5 9

7 56)9 8 5 6

8 38)7 6 0 0

9 40)8 0 4 0

10 48)7 2 9 6

11 55)9 7 3 5

12 53)7 2 0 8

13 62)9 6 1 0

14 62)9 7 3 4

15 51)7 9 5 6

16 45)9 4 0 5

@MathematicsByKim

-84-

Long Division

★ Challenge yourself
★ 2-Digit dividends
★ 2-Digit divisors

Date: ....

Name: ....

Score: ...... /16

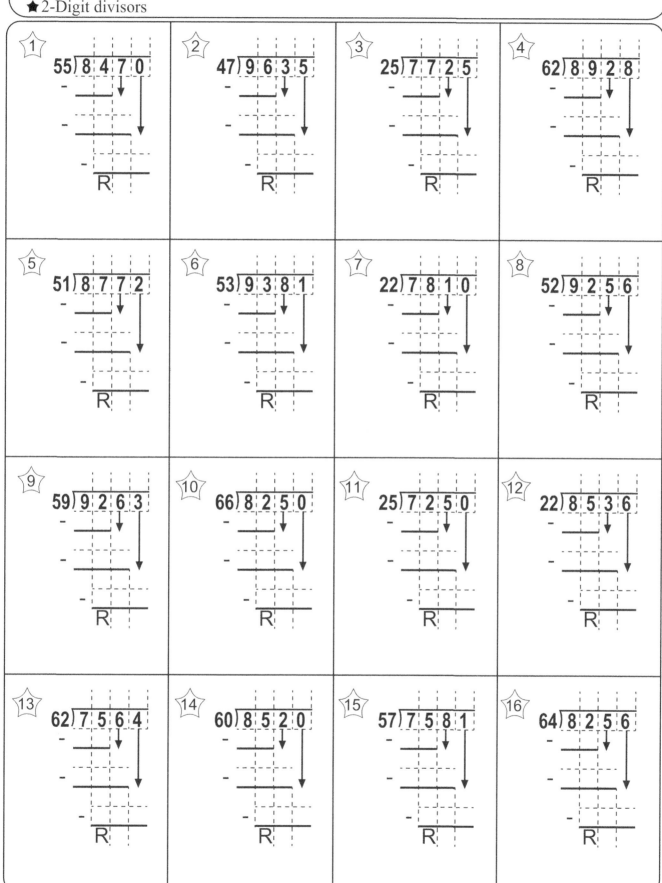

1   55)8 4 7 0

2   47)9 6 3 5

3   25)7 7 2 5

4   62)8 9 2 8

5   51)8 7 7 2

6   53)9 3 8 1

7   22)7 8 1 0

8   52)9 2 5 6

9   59)9 2 6 3

10   66)8 2 5 0

11   25)7 2 5 0

12   22)8 5 3 6

13   62)7 5 6 4

14   60)8 5 2 0

15   57)7 5 8 1

16   64)8 2 5 6

⟩ Long Division

★ Challenge yourself
★ 2-Digit dividends
★ 2-Digit divisors

Date: ....

Name: ....

Score: ...... /16

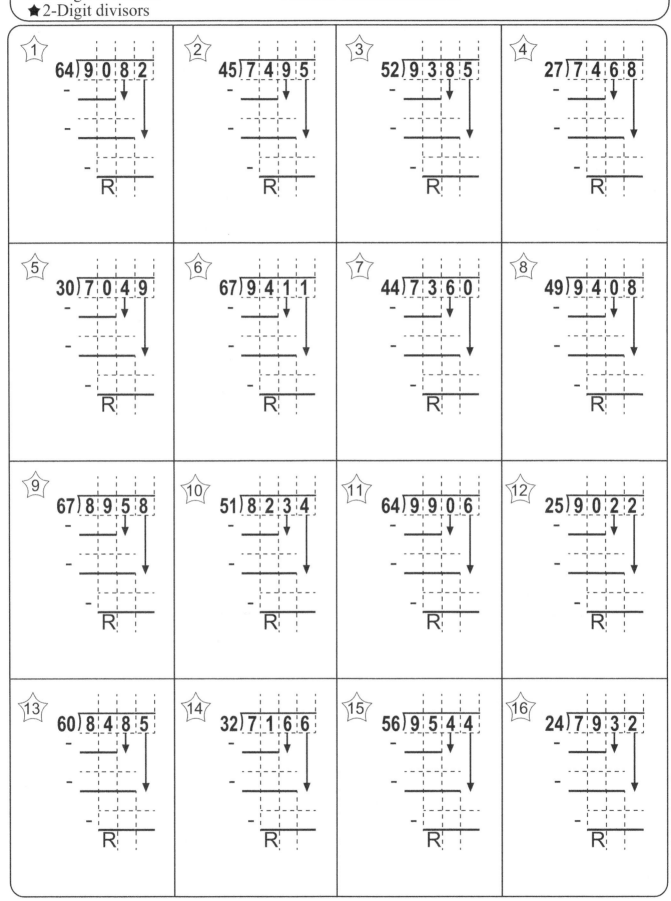

1   64 ⟩ 9 0 8 2

2   45 ⟩ 7 4 9 5

3   52 ⟩ 9 3 8 5

4   27 ⟩ 7 4 6 8

5   30 ⟩ 7 0 4 9

6   67 ⟩ 9 4 1 1

7   44 ⟩ 7 3 6 0

8   49 ⟩ 9 4 0 8

9   67 ⟩ 8 9 5 8

10   51 ⟩ 8 2 3 4

11   64 ⟩ 9 9 0 6

12   25 ⟩ 9 0 2 2

13   60 ⟩ 8 4 8 5

14   32 ⟩ 7 1 6 6

15   56 ⟩ 9 5 4 4

16   24 ⟩ 7 9 3 2

Long Division

★ Challenge yourself
★ 2-Digit dividends
★ 2-Digit divisors

Date: ....

Name: ....

Score: ...... /16

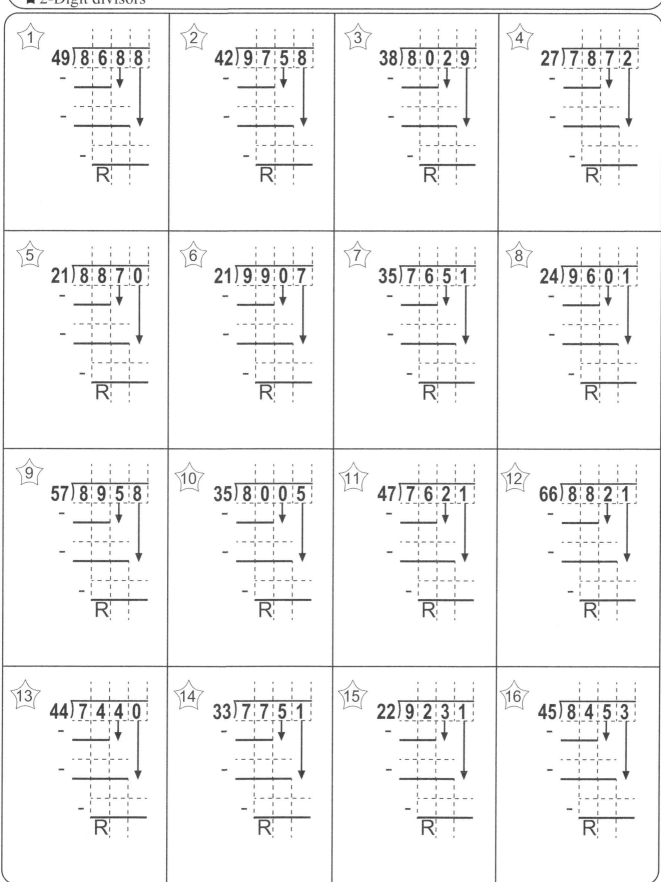

1. 49) 8 6 8 8

2. 42) 9 7 5 8

3. 38) 8 0 2 9

4. 27) 7 8 7 2

5. 21) 8 8 7 0

6. 21) 9 9 0 7

7. 35) 7 6 5 1

8. 24) 9 6 0 1

9. 57) 8 9 5 8

10. 35) 8 0 0 5

11. 47) 7 6 2 1

12. 66) 8 8 2 1

13. 44) 7 4 4 0

14. 33) 7 7 5 1

15. 22) 9 2 3 1

16. 45) 8 4 5 3

♪ Long Division
★ Challenge yourself
★ 2-Digit dividends
★ 2-Digit divisors

Date: ....

Name: ....

Score: ...... /16

1   59)9088

2   28)8056

3   27)8798

4   65)8490

5   30)8705

6   58)9912

7   37)8142

8   44)8483

9   44)8464

10 27)7293

11 34)8587

12 61)8117

13 25)7997

14 56)8156

15 37)8442

16 43)9635

)Long Division
★ Challenge yourself
★ 2-Digit dividends
★ 2-Digit divisors

Date: ....

Name: ....

Score: ...... /16

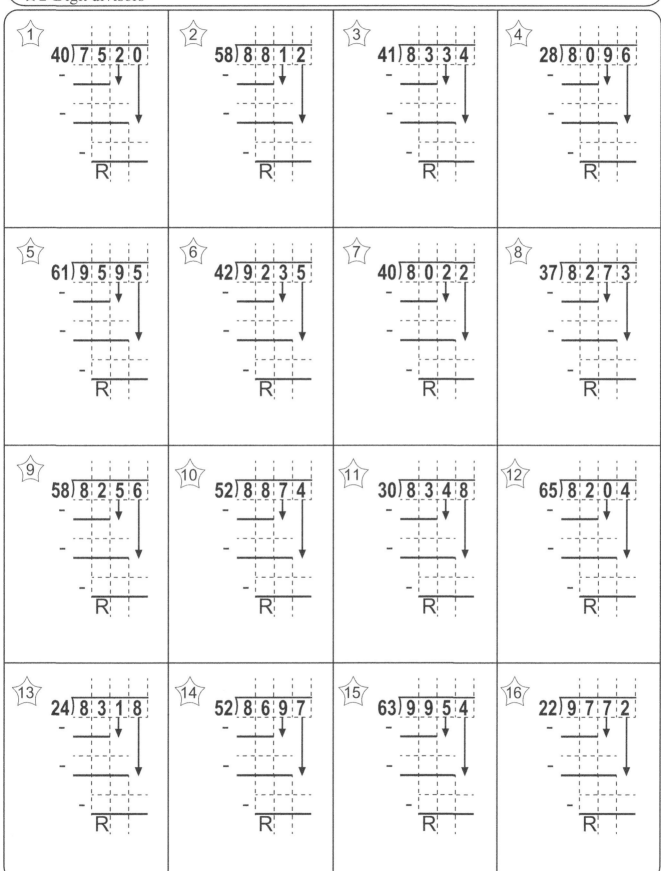

) Long Division

★ Challenge yourself
★ 2-Digit dividends
★ 2-Digit divisors

Date: ....

Name: ....

Score: ...... /16

1 32)8 6 9 3
R

2 21)8 7 0 2
R

3 22)7 2 1 9
R

4 55)9 0 8 8
R

5 35)8 4 2 3
R

6 46)8 9 9 1
R

7 44)8 5 6 5
R

8 64)9 0 2 2
R

9 49)8 9 3 6
R

10 34)8 2 4 4
R

11 29)9 4 2 4
R

12 67)7 7 8 5
R

13 55)9 1 4 6
R

14 22)8 5 5 4
R

15 26)9 7 1 9
R

16 36)8 8 1 9
R

Long Division
★ Challenge yourself
★ 2-Digit dividends
★ 2-Digit divisors

Date: ....

Name: ....

Score: ...... /16

1. 43)7 5 5 2 R

2. 58)8 9 2 6 R

3. 37)8 0 0 8 R

4. 37)9 7 6 6 R

5. 34)8 8 9 3 R

6. 27)7 5 2 2 R

7. 51)7 4 8 8 R

8. 42)7 9 8 9 R

9. 57)7 9 7 7 R

10. 27)8 0 1 0 R

11. 56)9 0 7 7 R

12. 43)7 9 7 6 R

13. 58)7 3 8 2 R

14. 64)7 5 2 0 R

15. 38)8 1 5 1 R

16. 41)8 9 0 3 R

⟩ Long Division

★ Challenge yourself
★ 2-Digit dividends
★ 2-Digit divisors

Date: ....

Name: ....

Score: ...... /16

1	51)9 3 3 8
2	54)7 9 9 4
3	52)7 6 5 8
4	54)7 4 8 4

5	55)9 9 4 0
6	50)9 2 2 9
7	69)9 0 6 1
8	24)9 4 1 7

9	25)7 9 8 1
10	65)8 1 1 5
11	28)7 8 8 1
12	54)9 5 1 4

13	52)8 1 5 3
14	30)9 2 3 1
15	23)8 2 5 1
16	70)8 6 5 9

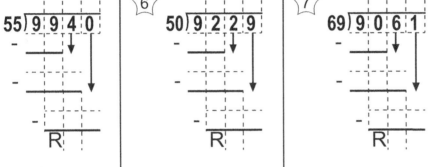
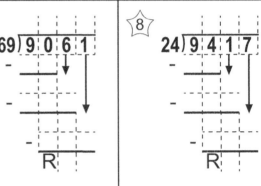
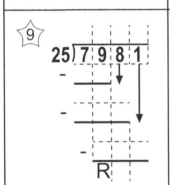
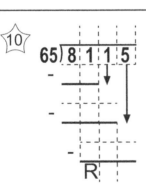
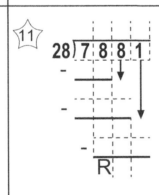
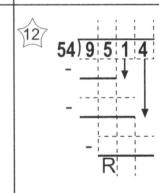
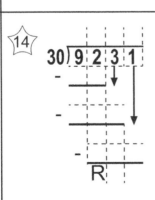
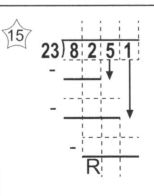

Long Division
★ Challenge yourself
★ 2-Digit dividends
★ 2-Digit divisors

Date: ....

Name: ....

Score: ...... /16

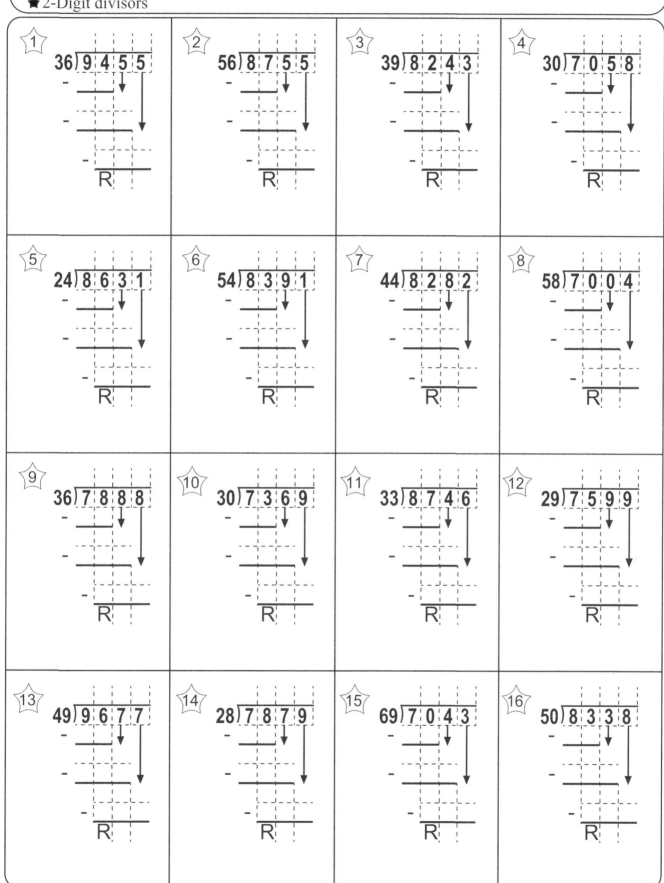

) Long Division
★ Challenge yourself
★ 2-Digit dividends
★ 2-Digit divisors

Date: ....

Name: ....

Score: ...... /16

1	59) 9 8 1 4
2	64) 8 8 2 8
3	49) 7 9 1 5
4	50) 9 5 2 3

R

5	47) 9 0 8 0
6	49) 9 9 2 8
7	69) 8 2 9 9
8	53) 8 2 2 8

R

9	24) 8 5 1 2
10	66) 9 1 5 5
11	40) 7 2 6 5
12	48) 7 2 8 5

R

13	41) 7 3 3 2
14	62) 9 4 6 1
15	63) 7 2 5 9
16	48) 7 5 6 7

R

@MathematicsByKim

-94-

ANSWERS

Page 1:

1] 14   2] 22   3] 15   4] 19   5] 18   6] 41   7] 13   8] 23   9] 27   10] 18

11] 11   12] 26   13] 17   14] 10   15] 14   16] 48

Page 2:

1] 17   2] 31   3] 24   4] 16   5] 36   6] 14   7] 25   8] 12   9] 21   10] 13

11] 17   12] 44   13] 16   14] 24   15] 10   16] 21

Page 3:

1] 46   2] 17   3] 27   4] 16   5] 10   6] 23   7] 12   8] 11   9] 20   10] 24

11] 15   12] 15   13] 23   14] 12   15] 30   16] 29

Page 4:

1] 23   2] 17   3] 19   4] 23   5] 18   6] 30   7] 21   8] 27   9] 15   10] 21

11] 31   12] 19   13] 11   14] 20   15] 15   16] 31

Page 5:

1] 31   2] 13   3] 23   4] 12   5] 17   6] 18   7] 19   8] 10   9] 13   10] 30

11] 18   12] 19   13] 17   14] 48   15] 22   16] 27

Page 6:

1] 24 R3   2] 15 R3   3] 14 R2   4] 20 R2   5] 14 R5   6] 19 R4   7] 18 R4

8] 20 R3   9] 12 R4   10] 26 R0   11] 16 R2   12] 18 R1   13] 14 R4   14] 47 R0

15] 25 R2   16] 17 R3

Page 7:

1] 11 R2   2] 41 R0   3] 15 R2   4] 13 R3   5] 19 R1   6] 45 R1   7] 28 R1

8] 16 R3   9] 13 R2   10] 39 R0   11] 21 R2   12] 30 R2   13] 14 R4   14] 18 R2

15] 17 R3   16] 19 R0

Page 8:

1] 13 R4   2] 28 R1   3] 12 R1   4] 12 R6   5] 41 R1   6] 16 R0   7] 32 R0

8] 47 R1   9] 25 R0   10] 28 R2   11] 13 R0   12] 26 R2   13] 49 R1   14] 15 R5

15] 13 R4   16] 15 R4

Page 9:

1] 11 R3   2] 15 R4   3] 21 R1   4] 23 R3   5] 18 R1   6] 15 R3   7] 25 R2

8] 16 R0   9] 13 R1   10] 14 R1   11] 11 R0   12] 18 R3   13] 15 R0   14] 18 R0

15] 15 R2   16] 38 R0

@MathematicsByKim

Page 10:
1] 15 R0   2] 24 R0   3] 17 R4   4] 13 R5   5] 10 R3   6] 19 R0   7] 25 R1

8] 16 R2   9] 22 R0   10] 12 R6   11] 22 R1   12] 23 R2   13] 13 R0   14] 44 R1

15] 30 R1   16] 27 R2

Page 11:
1] 226   2] 154   3] 152   4] 119   5] 147   6] 161   7] 133   8] 248   9] 164

10] 129   11] 144   12] 194   13] 195   14] 210   15] 244   16] 158

Page 12:
1] 325   2] 127   3] 405   4] 442   5] 179   6] 118   7] 151   8] 212   9] 257

10] 200   11] 131   12] 331   13] 121   14] 220   15] 160   16] 412

Page 13:
1] 143   2] 213   3] 249   4] 424   5] 125   6] 229   7] 274   8] 211   9] 468

10] 187   11] 131   12] 179   13] 181   14] 137   15] 147   16] 153

Page 14:
1] 137   2] 233   3] 238   4] 159   5] 219   6] 252   7] 285   8] 175   9] 242

10] 157   11] 133   12] 135   13] 292   14] 227   15] 120   16] 152

Page 15:
1] 370   2] 209   3] 137   4] 325   5] 160   6] 133   7] 123   8] 149   9] 277

10] 278   11] 162   12] 441   13] 121   14] 135   15] 261   16] 171

Page 16:
1] 144   2] 109   3] 200   4] 171   5] 134   6] 205   7] 155   8] 184   9] 378

10] 396   11] 209   12] 130   13] 150   14] 246   15] 250   16] 187

Page 17:
1] 135   2] 258   3] 228   4] 412   5] 460   6] 220   7] 243   8] 121   9] 185

10] 299   11] 167   12] 165   13] 296   14] 151   15] 302   16] 172

Page 18:
1] 290   2] 297   3] 164   4] 234   5] 177   6] 456   7] 101   8] 187   9] 122

10] 246   11] 211   12] 199   13] 134   14] 172   15] 287   16] 117

Page 19:
1] 139   2] 147   3] 247   4] 200   5] 475   6] 108   7] 139   8] 189   9] 165

10] 127   11] 143   12] 141   13] 170   14] 240   15] 389   16] 125

@MathematicsByKim

Page 20:

1] 309   2] 145   3] 179   4] 212   5] 100   6] 158   7] 131   8] 258   9] 395

10] 304   11] 141   12] 234   13] 164   14] 288   15] 235   16] 193

Page 21:

1] 172   2] 115   3] 284   4] 168   5] 167   6] 184   7] 211   8] 174   9] 215

10] 118   11] 337   12] 133   13] 180   14] 226   15] 161   16] 212

Page 22:

1] 118   2] 222   3] 252   4] 239   5] 168   6] 200   7] 314   8] 298   9] 216

10] 209   11] 290   12] 205   13] 231   14] 142   15] 182   16] 227

Page 23:

1] 222   2] 108   3] 202   4] 281   5] 154   6] 210   7] 221   8] 104   9] 248

10] 151   11] 183   12] 327   13] 120   14] 192   15] 227   16] 228

Page 24:

1] 219   2] 162   3] 230   4] 133   5] 161   6] 206   7] 301   8] 342   9] 181

10] 103   11] 213   12] 111   13] 154   14] 169   15] 158   16] 109

Page 25:

1] 128   2] 118   3] 148   4] 124   5] 101   6] 148   7] 106   8] 105   9] 141

10] 130   11] 103   12] 101   13] 107   14] 121   15] 105   16] 151

Page 26:

1] 106   2] 108   3] 104   4] 127   5] 149   6] 123   7] 149   8] 133   9] 127

10] 126   11] 111   12] 118   13] 134   14] 134   15] 127   16] 112

Page 27:

1] 115   2] 102   3] 100   4] 117   5] 133   6] 139   7] 138   8] 114   9] 123

10] 117   11] 137   12] 121   13] 132   14] 110   15] 103   16] 136

Page 28:

1] 143 R4   2] 331 R2   3] 120 R1   4] 133 R4   5] 161 R4   6] 189 R1

7] 455 R1   8] 153 R4   9] 330 R2   10] 165 R3   11] 232 R2   12] 180 R0

13] 188 R0   14] 144 R4   15] 231 R3   16] 264 R2

Page 29:

1] 163 R3   2] 186 R0   3] 161 R4   4] 122 R2   5] 191 R3   6] 164 R4

7] 181 R3   8] 188 R0   9] 152 R2   10] 227 R3   11] 160 R4   12] 193 R4

13] 498 R0   14] 148 R2   15] 263 R0   16] 368 R1

@MathematicsByKim

Page 30:

1] 489 R1	2] 481 R1	3] 493 R1	4] 196 R2	5] 302 R2	6] 188 R1
7] 125 R5	8] 244 R2	9] 114 R3	10] 260 R0	11] 239 R2	12] 142 R0
13] 161 R0	14] 159 R1	15] 416 R1	16] 410 R0		

Page 31:

1] 163 R3	2] 107 R3	3] 284 R1	4] 429 R1	5] 289 R2	6] 182 R0
7] 299 R0	8] 151 R0	9] 243 R2	10] 190 R2	11] 173 R1	12] 148 R4
13] 297 R2	14] 239 R1	15] 240 R1	16] 156 R0		

Page 32:

1] 188 R3	2] 295 R1	3] 128 R2	4] 134 R3	5] 319 R2	6] 157 R4
7] 117 R4	8] 320 R2	9] 224 R0	10] 240 R0	11] 114 R1	12] 151 R4
13] 150 R0	14] 227 R1	15] 209 R1	16] 115 R6		

Page 33:

1] 123 R4	2] 138 R1	3] 326 R2	4] 196 R3	5] 251 R0	6] 165 R4
7] 291 R2	8] 241 R2	9] 325 R2	10] 162 R2	11] 156 R2	12] 145 R0
13] 273 R2	14] 324 R1	15] 270 R2	16] 165 R4		

Page 34:

1] 117 R2	2] 291 R2	3] 146 R5	4] 262 R0	5] 186 R2	6] 451 R0
7] 452 R0	8] 421 R1	9] 178 R0	10] 494 R1	11] 295 R1	12] 244 R2
13] 458 R1	14] 352 R0	15] 182 R0	16] 236 R0		

Page 35:

1] 101 R2	2] 218 R3	3] 100 R6	4] 252 R0	5] 326 R0	6] 129 R5
7] 295 R2	8] 287 R2	9] 324 R1	10] 303 R0	11] 107 R0	12] 481 R1
13] 270 R2	14] 135 R5	15] 253 R1	16] 458 R0		

Page 36:

1] 146 R1	2] 185 R3	3] 232 R2	4] 147 R0	5] 168 R3	6] 201 R3
7] 175 R2	8] 175 R1	9] 137 R0	10] 175 R3	11] 129 R2	12] 149 R4
13] 318 R2	14] 377 R0	15] 225 R2	16] 184 R4		

Page 37:

1] 198 R1	2] 132 R0	3] 182 R3	4] 234 R1	5] 265 R0	6] 133 R4
7] 167 R3	8] 119 R4	9] 133 R0	10] 140 R1	11] 491 R1	12] 148 R1
13] 188 R2	14] 112 R2	15] 224 R0	16] 306 R2		

Page 38:

1] 222 R0   2] 321 R0   3] 164 R1   4] 153 R2   5] 130 R1   6] 245 R1

7] 231 R0   8] 200 R2   9] 183 R1   10] 242 R1   11] 118 R0   12] 114 R3

13] 215 R2   14] 130 R3   15] 214 R1   16] 170 R3

Page 39:

1] 243 R0   2] 191 R2   3] 127 R1   4] 158 R2   5] 186 R2   6] 258 R1

7] 172 R2   8] 190 R1   9] 246 R1   10] 151 R1   11] 208 R0   12] 168 R2

13] 211 R1   14] 216 R2   15] 136 R1   16] 227 R1

Page 40:

1] 235 R1   2] 175 R0   3] 170 R1   4] 142 R0   5] 322 R1   6] 233 R0

7] 180 R1   8] 196 R2   9] 234 R1   10] 261 R2   11] 205 R0   12] 222 R1

13] 155 R0   14] 221 R1   15] 221 R2   16] 198 R0

Page 41:

1] 279 R1   2] 183 R2   3] 223 R1   4] 225 R2   5] 180 R1   6] 216 R1

7] 213 R1   8] 198 R3   9] 288 R1   10] 147 R0   11] 254 R1   12] 387 R1

13] 101 R3   14] 357 R0   15] 138 R2   16] 154 R1

Page 42:

1] 143 R0   2] 180 R3   3] 144 R3   4] 118 R0   5] 155 R0   6] 100 R6

7] 146 R0   8] 166 R2   9] 115 R4   10] 101 R5   11] 179 R1   12] 161 R4

13] 134 R4   14] 164 R1   15] 129 R5   16] 153 R5

Page 43:

1] 100 R4   2] 115 R5   3] 108 R5   4] 146 R5   5] 138 R5   6] 150 R1

7] 148 R5   8] 149 R5   9] 141 R3   10] 115 R5   11] 108 R0   12] 121 R6

13] 121 R3   14] 128 R5   15] 142 R0   16] 140 R3

Page 44:

1] 139 R0   2] 103 R4   3] 121 R3   4] 118 R0   5] 119 R7   6] 124 R6

7] 128 R6   8] 104 R2   9] 102 R0   10] 100 R5   11] 123 R7   12] 123 R6

13] 110 R6   14] 138 R4   15] 140 R2   16] 107 R4

Page 45:

1] 1485   2] 1424   3] 4009   4] 4034   5] 1205   6] 4649   7] 3319   8] 1246

9] 1860   10] 1989   11] 1884   12] 2476   13] 1622   14] 1954   15] 2338   16] 1318

@MathematicsByKim

Page 46:

1] 4176   2] 1336   3] 2572   4] 3940   5] 1709   6] 1528   7] 4283   8] 3007

9] 1134   10] 3098   11] 1349   12] 1358   13] 1418   14] 1474   15] 1251   16] 3009

Page 47:

1] 2526   2] 1284   3] 4356   4] 1498   5] 1953   6] 2994   7] 2066   8] 3596

9] 3249   10] 1776   11] 1436   12] 4221   13] 1979   14] 1424   15] 1630   16] 1427

Page 48:

1] 1103   2] 2599   3] 3551   4] 2454   5] 1654   6] 2410   7] 1042   8] 1801

9] 2841   10] 1260   11] 2389   12] 4706   13] 2934   14] 1420   15] 1438   16] 1498

Page 49:

1] 1608   2] 1225   3] 1468   4] 1438   5] 3318   6] 1611   7] 1636   8] 2674

9] 4831   10] 1027   11] 4750   12] 1852   13] 2300   14] 1198   15] 1431   16] 1107

Page 50:

1] 1249   2] 1583   3] 4717   4] 2891   5] 2259   6] 1816   7] 1484   8] 1825

9] 3662   10] 1231   11] 1687   12] 1365   13] 2806   14] 2788   15] 2834   16] 1814

Page 51:

1] 2689   2] 3612   3] 2399   4] 2361   5] 1986   6] 3051   7] 1611   8] 1989

9] 1215   10] 1438   11] 1362   12] 1821   13] 3773   14] 1710   15] 2472   16] 2159

Page 52:

1] 1713   2] 1440   3] 1899   4] 1434   5] 1400   6] 2399   7] 1426   8] 1548

9] 2207   10] 3622   11] 1294   12] 1557   13] 2029   14] 2640   15] 1479   16] 3125

Page 53:

1] 2457   2] 3328   3] 1449   4] 2121   5] 1424   6] 1920   7] 1443   8] 4292

9] 1441   10] 2400   11] 2095   12] 2379   13] 2940   14] 3827   15] 1622   16] 1507

Page 54:

1] 1075   2] 1889   3] 1516   4] 3099   5] 1960   6] 1632   7] 3279   8] 4376

9] 3056   10] 1963   11] 1117   12] 4340   13] 1329   14] 1392   15] 1786   16] 1938

Page 55:

1] 2555   2] 1806   3] 2548   4] 1770   5] 3286   6] 1302   7] 1525   8] 1370

9] 1745   10] 1648   11] 1452   12] 2603   13] 1440   14] 2271   15] 2575   16] 3035

Page 56:

1] 2640   2] 2128   3] 2137   4] 1348   5] 3569   6] 1812   7] 1826   8] 2185

9] 2578   10] 2585   11] 2464   12] 2238   13] 2159   14] 2152   15] 1313   16] 1514

Page 57:

1] 3689   2] 1385   3] 2192   4] 1680   5] 2267   6] 2104   7] 2294   8] 2433

9] 2282   10] 3348   11] 1442   12] 1985   13] 1405   14] 3406   15] 2618   16] 3706

Page 58:

1] 2313   2] 2737   3] 1866   4] 1953   5] 1961   6] 2300   7] 2605   8] 1315

9] 1778   10] 2374   11] 2383   12] 2232   13] 1817   14] 2469   15] 2008   16] 2396

Page 59:

1] 1483   2] 1403   3] 1168   4] 1401   5] 1367   6] 1435   7] 1164   8] 1246

9] 1166   10] 1096   11] 1235   12] 1509   13] 1340   14] 1378   15] 1215   16] 1204

Page 60:

1] 1418   2] 1000   3] 1072   4] 1005   5] 1268   6] 1378   7] 1229   8] 1221

9] 1139   10] 1060   11] 1425   12] 1173   13] 1189   14] 1235   15] 1220   16] 1149

Page 61:

1] 1006   2] 1063   3] 1197   4] 1134   5] 1017   6] 1206   7] 1002   8] 1201

9] 1166   10] 1164   11] 1181   12] 1098   13] 1020   14] 1073   15] 1246   16] 1086

Page 62:

1] 1066 R4   2] 2315 R3   3] 4397 R1   4] 1245 R4   5] 1312 R1   6] 2357 R2

7] 2216 R0   8] 1225 R2   9] 2225 R3   10] 4588 R0   11] 1626 R4   12] 1902 R3

13] 1541 R1   14] 1541 R3   15] 1251 R1   16] 4247 R0

Page 63:

1] 1575 R0   2] 2231 R2   3] 3856 R1   4] 1329 R4   5] 1282 R5   6] 2574 R1

7] 4840 R0   8] 1359 R4   9] 2556 R1   10] 1388 R0   11] 2193 R0   12] 1332 R0

13] 1652 R1   14] 3079 R2   15] 3032 R2   16] 1334 R5

Page 64:

1] 1436 R4   2] 4507 R1   3] 1430 R4   4] 2356 R3   5] 1911 R3   6] 1592 R3

7] 1402 R0   8] 1520 R1   9] 4309 R0   10] 1924 R4   11] 2353 R2   12] 1421 R2

13] 4631 R1   14] 1371 R0   15] 1983 R2   16] 4917 R0

Page 65:

1] 1498 R0   2] 1903 R3   3] 1100 R1   4] 2028 R0   5] 1873 R3   6] 3698 R1

7] 1183 R4   8] 2219 R3   9] 4207 R0   10] 1267 R2   11] 1589 R2   12] 1839 R0

13] 3740 R0   14] 1287 R4   15] 1262 R2   16] 1493 R2

Page 66:

1] 1536 R0	2] 1604 R4	3] 1865 R1	4] 2544 R1	5] 1746 R2	6] 1477 R3
7] 1755 R1	8] 1604 R1	9] 1597 R2	10] 4217 R0	11] 4962 R0	12] 2385 R0
13] 2065 R3	14] 3607 R0	15] 4192 R1	16] 1888 R0		

Page 67:

1] 2794 R0	2] 1613 R1	3] 3833 R0	4] 2489 R2	5] 2294 R0	6] 1135 R5
7] 2841 R1	8] 2030 R3	9] 2196 R0	10] 1068 R6	11] 2319 R1	12] 3153 R2
13] 3111 R0	14] 1468 R2	15] 1518 R4	16] 1612 R1		

Page 68:

1] 1628 R5	2] 1314 R0	3] 2978 R2	4] 2312 R2	5] 2460 R1	6] 1851 R4
7] 2256 R3	8] 1785 R0	9] 2910 R0	10] 2668 R0	11] 1212 R3	12] 1392 R5
13] 1031 R5	14] 1745 R2	15] 2424 R2	16] 3926 R0		

Page 69:

1] 1574 R4	2] 2737 R1	3] 1298 R1	4] 1893 R2	5] 2488 R3	6] 1523 R2
7] 1053 R0	8] 1451 R3	9] 1498 R3	10] 4982 R0	11] 1365 R1	12] 2054 R0
13] 1499 R1	14] 2449 R3	15] 1595 R4	16] 1568 R3		

Page 70:

1] 1260 R3	2] 4369 R0	3] 1772 R2	4] 2427 R1	5] 2289 R3	6] 1416 R1
7] 4653 R0	8] 4838 R0	9] 1403 R1	10] 2809 R0	11] 1724 R0	12] 4089 R0
13] 1174 R5	14] 1182 R5	15] 1505 R0	16] 2347 R3		

Page 71:

1] 1667 R2	2] 1053 R5	3] 3030 R0	4] 1319 R5	5] 2384 R3	6] 3885 R1
7] 1179 R5	8] 1192 R1	9] 2800 R2	10] 1790 R2	11] 1956 R0	12] 1997 R0
13] 2107 R0	14] 1300 R4	15] 2193 R3	16] 1367 R5		

Page 72:

1] 1311 R0	2] 2187 R0	3] 3753 R0	4] 1559 R1	5] 1737 R1	6] 3021 R0
7] 3647 R0	8] 2142 R0	9] 3467 R1	10] 2371 R1	11] 1729 R0	12] 1431 R3
13] 1941 R0	14] 1071 R3	15] 2281 R0	16] 1405 R0		

Page 73:

1] 2640 R1	2] 3960 R1	3] 2122 R0	4] 1679 R0	5] 2568 R1	6] 2957 R1
7] 3914 R0	8] 1865 R1	9] 2000 R1	10] 1920 R0	11] 3283 R0	12] 1089 R0
13] 2435 R2	14] 2053 R2	15] 1966 R1	16] 2715 R0		

Page 74:

1] 2532 R0   2] 2939 R1   3] 3125 R1   4] 1826 R0   5] 2350 R0   6] 1188 R2

7] 2449 R1   8] 1793 R2   9] 3291 R0   10] 1271 R3   11] 1347 R2   12] 2060 R2

13] 2590 R1   14] 3010 R0   15] 1578 R0   16] 1503 R2

Page 75:

1] 2891 R1   2] 2486 R2   3] 3380 R1   4] 2316 R1   5] 1264 R0   6] 1937 R2

7] 2096 R2   8] 2583 R1   9] 1068 R2   10] 2272 R0   11] 1533 R0   12] 1474 R3

13] 1658 R0   14] 1171 R2   15] 1167 R1   16] 3574 R1

Page 76:

1] 1172 R1   2] 1405 R4   3] 1548 R5   4] 1299 R2   5] 1458 R3   6] 1419 R2

7] 1388 R0   8] 1099 R0   9] 1316 R3   10] 1192 R4   11] 1643 R2   12] 1633 R3

13] 1453 R0   14] 1605 R1   15] 1205 R3   16] 1173 R4

Page 77:

1] 1076 R7   2] 1165 R1   3] 1343 R2   4] 1152 R5   5] 1170 R1   6] 1113 R7

7] 1020 R6   8] 1097 R3   9] 1098 R3   10] 1162 R0   11] 1234 R4   12] 1369 R4

13] 1379 R4   14] 1121 R4   15] 1336 R5   16] 1309 R4

Page 78:

1] 1072 R5   2] 1002 R3   3] 1242 R0   4] 1202 R4   5] 1133 R5   6] 1013 R2

7] 1156 R0   8] 1099 R8   9] 1146 R2   10] 1162 R3   11] 1019 R8   12] 1233 R7

13] 1055 R3   14] 1086 R4   15] 1014 R8   16] 1073 R5

Page 79:

1] 180   2] 371   3] 121   4] 175   5] 144   6] 193   7] 118   8] 246   9] 465

10] 156   11] 258   12] 154   13] 414   14] 302   15] 139   16] 119

Page 80:

1] 107   2] 311   3] 188   4] 273   5] 341   6] 207   7] 217   8] 266   9] 121

10] 120   11] 182   12] 141   13] 209   14] 215   15] 218   16] 230

Page 81:

1] 161   2] 208   3] 158   4] 153   5] 200   6] 166   7] 144   8] 487   9] 220

10] 204   11] 368   12] 135   13] 251   14] 127   15] 341   16] 373

Page 82:

1] 333   2] 357   3] 130   4] 283   5] 237   6] 139   7] 155   8] 225   9] 124

10] 167   11] 147   12] 372   13] 126   14] 186   15] 331   16] 242

@MathematicsByKim

Page 83:

1] 233   2] 156   3] 133   4] 482   5] 333   6] 117   7] 166   8] 410   9] 242

10] 154   11] 404   12] 270   13] 143   14] 173   15] 134   16] 285

Page 84:

1] 193   2] 230   3] 175   4] 285   5] 192   6] 111   7] 176   8] 200   9] 201

10] 152   11] 177   12] 136   13] 155   14] 157   15] 156   16] 209

Page 85:

1] 154   2] 205   3] 309   4] 144   5] 172   6] 177   7] 355   8] 178   9] 157

10] 125   11] 290   12] 388   13] 122   14] 142   15] 133   16] 129

Page 86:

1] 141 R58   2] 166 R25   3] 180 R25   4] 276 R16   5] 234 R29   6] 140 R31

7] 167 R12   8] 192 R0   9] 133 R47   10] 161 R23   11] 154 R50   12] 360 R22

13] 141 R25   14] 223 R30   15] 170 R24   16] 330 R12

Page 87:

1] 177 R15   2] 232 R14   3] 211 R11   4] 291 R15   5] 422 R8   6] 471 R16

7] 218 R21   8] 400 R1   9] 157 R9   10] 228 R25   11] 162 R7   12] 133 R43

13] 169 R4   14] 234 R29   15] 419 R13   16] 187 R38

Page 88:

1] 154 R2   2] 287 R20   3] 325 R23   4] 130 R40   5] 290 R5   6] 170 R52

7] 220 R2   8] 192 R35   9] 192 R16   10] 270 R3   11] 252 R19   12] 133 R4

13] 319 R22   14] 145 R36   15] 228 R6   16] 224 R3

Page 89:

1] 188 R0   2] 151 R54   3] 203 R11   4] 289 R4   5] 157 R18   6] 219 R37

7] 200 R22   8] 223 R22   9] 142 R20   10] 170 R34   11] 278 R8   12] 126 R14

13] 346 R14   14] 167 R13   15] 158 R0   16] 444 R4

Page 90:

1] 271 R21   2] 414 R8   3] 328 R3   4] 165 R13   5] 240 R23   6] 195 R21

7] 194 R29   8] 140 R62   9] 182 R18   10] 242 R16   11] 324 R28   12] 116 R13

13] 166 R16   14] 388 R18   15] 373 R21   16] 244 R35

Page 91:

1] 175 R27   2] 153 R52   3] 216 R16   4] 263 R35   5] 261 R19   6] 278 R16

7] 146 R42   8] 190 R9   9] 139 R54   10] 296 R18   11] 162 R5   12] 185 R21

@MathematicsByKim

13] 127 R16   14] 117 R32   15] 214 R19   16] 217 R6

Page 92:

1] 183 R5   2] 148 R2   3] 147 R14   4] 138 R32   5] 180 R40   6] 184 R29

7] 131 R22   8] 392 R9   9] 319 R6   10] 124 R55   11] 281 R13   12] 176 R10

13] 156 R41   14] 307 R21   15] 358 R17   16] 123 R49

Page 93:

1] 262 R23   2] 156 R19   3] 211 R14   4] 235 R8   5] 359 R15   6] 155 R21

7] 188 R10   8] 120 R44   9] 219 R4   10] 245 R19   11] 265 R1   12] 262 R1

13] 197 R24   14] 281 R11   15] 102 R5   16] 166 R38

Page 94:

1] 166 R20   2] 137 R60   3] 161 R26   4] 190 R23   5] 193 R9   6] 202 R30

7] 120 R19   8] 155 R13   9] 354 R16   10] 138 R47   11] 181 R25   12] 151 R37

13] 178 R34   14] 152 R37   15] 115 R14   16] 157 R31

Made in the USA
Las Vegas, NV
10 October 2024

96585103R00063